The Safest Place in the World

The Safest Place in the World
A PERSONAL HISTORY OF BRITISH RHYTHM AND BLUES

Dick Heckstall-Smith

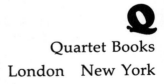

Quartet Books

London   New York

First published by Quartet Books Limited 1989
A member of the Namara Group
27/29 Goodge Street, London W1P 1FD

Copyright © 1989 by Dick Heckstall-Smith
Cartoons © Biff 1989

British Library Cataloguing in Publication Data

Heckstall-Smith, Dick
The safest place in the world.
1. Great Britain. Blues, 1960–1970.
Biographies
I. Title
784.5'3'00924

ISBN 0–7043–2696–5

Typeset by MC Typeset Ltd, Gillingham
Printed and bound in Great Britain by
BPCC Hazell Books Ltd
Member of BPCC Ltd
Aylesbury, Bucks, England

Contents

Preface *by Jack Bruce*   vii

Foreword   xi

1   Fledgling   1
2   Substances   13
3   Blues Incorporated   32
4   The Beginning of the Graham Bond
    Organization   45
5   Snowed In   58
6   To be a Ruined Man is Itself a Vocation   65
7   The End of the Graham Bond Organization   81
8   Interregnum: John Mayall's Bluesbreakers   86
9   The Rise of Colosseum   100
10   'Jon Hiseman's Clothes Museum' –
    Dave Greenslade   114
11   Why Did Colosseum Fall?   124
12   A Story Ended   135

Afterword: Race and Racism in Music   144

Chronology   155

Discography   158

Index   171

Preface

I remember walking through the still innocent Soho of 1962, in the wake of the longer, Gordonstounian legs of Dick Heckstall-Smith: echoes of walks taken with my father through the Glasgow of ten years before. As it happened, Dick was my musical father.

.It was around this time that Dick, Ginger Baker and myself formed an experimental trio which played an almost exclusive resonancy in Dick's basement flat in Miranda Road. One tune of Dick's that we played, 'The Tube', gave me a musical 'philosophy' almost on its own. This was also when Dick became known as the Rowing Captain: he was responsible for more esoteric musicians joining bands than I think he knows.

I was rowed into Alexis Korner's band. When I first heard Blues Incorporated at the Marquee, my initial feeling was indignation: 'It's just a rock'n'roll band.' I was the victim of a bad case of jazz snobbery, and joining this band did more to broaden my musical outlook (I was not alone) than anything or anyone, until Robert Johnson came along.

The ten years that followed, a good part of them spent in Bedford vans of one denomination or another, may seem a bit of a blur to me – but luckily Dick remembers.

Yes, he has got the flavour. The feeling of wasting time while not having a moment to lose. Hurry up to Manchester, a famous Tubby Hayes belch. Being so bored that you ended up eating daffodils. The secret of the junky's clandestine fix; the antithesis of what happens in room 101 – the best, the safest thing in the world. It was in those vans that Dick would crack his gum, and the spine of *Under the Volcano*, and say – very little. If he was in a state of transition, the rest of us were in one of excess.

But there is little doubt that the years spent in the Graham Bond Organization were vital to those of us who survived. Dick compares those days and nights with serving your time at a factory bench, or perhaps more like National Service. I think of them as my time at university. In much the same way that physical exercise practised in youth will sustain you later on, there is almost no tour today, no matter how gruelling, that seems hard in comparison with those days. No gig too far. We made our album *Sound of '65* in one three-hour session – recording two of my earliest songs in the last twenty minutes – including overdubs, between hundreds of performances.

After my departure – at the wrong end of a knife – from the GBO (perhaps a better name might have been GBH), I saw less of Dick than I would have liked; that kind of love forged by the intensity of shared experience dies hard. With the exception of a famous night at the 100 Club, and the fortunate recording we made together with Jon Hiseman and John McLaughlin in 1968, we had become strangers until about five years ago, when yet again he rowed me into a gig. This time it was with Norman Beaker's band in Manchester. I was amazed at the way Dick had perfected his art. He had become the most consummate blues horn player I'd ever heard. With the aid of some very complicated and sinister-looking pedals and electronic devices, he was able to imbue his solos with a sound and feeling of rightness, of inevitability: the kind associated with another great blues improviser, Little Walter.

And it is not only in music that Dick has continued to develop since his quiet, uncommitted days in Graham Bond's vans. I sometimes wonder if the vaguely political conversations, mainly between Ginger and me, that went down during those interminable pre-motorway journeys had something to do with it.

A few years after this time, following the souring of Cream, I was accused, in the musical press by Eric Clapton, of being 'too angry'. It has taken Dick a little time, but by the last chapter of this book he is describing the birth of a healthy, practical, political awareness, arguably the more valid for being arrived at by other means than the purely emotional. Today, thank Marx, it has developed into a fine, smouldering anger.

There is no doubt in my mind that we will make more excursions together – and I hope to do the walking.

Jack Bruce

Foreword

The scene: Ray's Record Shop, Shaftesbury Avenue. The time: just before Christmas 1984. I was ferreting around for Bessie Smith, who was a powerful Christmas present that year. I'd just found what I was after when I was accosted by a bloke I'd met, so far as I knew, once before, and that briefly: a lively, burly character in, I judged, his early forties, with penetrating near-black eyes. He was a publisher, he said, and how would I like to write a book? A *book*? I was puzzled. What about? About anything you like, of course, he said skilfully – but how about your life in music? And he invited me to come and discuss it in a place he knew round the corner. By the time we left that coffee house I was already forming plans. This is the result of William Pryor's bearding of Dick Heckstall-Smith, courtesy of Ray Smith and the Monmouth Coffee House. Thank you, William.

I've always assumed that writing autobiography was pretty much child's play: you don't have to invent anything or discover anything, you just have to write down what happened. Now I know different. The problem is to *not* invent anything . . .

What's involved is the great 'If I'd Known Then What I Know Now' principle: the author of autobiography isn't quite the person who lived through the events he's writing about. The temptation is subtly to change the flavour of what happened in the light of what the writer feels about it now. The line I've taken is to do no research to speak of, nor to dredge too deeply into obscure memories, but to write as well as I can about what comes freely to mind. I'm aware that this approach leaves a lot out. I never kept a diary apart from for names, phone numbers, appointments and so on, and a great deal has sunk without trace, perhaps for ever. What I do remember, however, I've written about without, so far as I know, inventing anything. Whatever its disadvantages, this way of going about things has minimized any tendency to smuggle the author's present attitudes into what happened in, say, 1959.

All the same I would dearly like to know: do all writers walk about their homes at a quarter to five in the morning with their heads sunk on their chests, laughing and groaning and whispering to themselves?

I want to thank the following people for their valuable aid and encouragement: Danny Adler, Pete Bailey Senior, Ginger Baker, Margaret Bluman, Jack Bruce, Eileen Cadman, Dave Clempson, Janet Godfrey, Peter Gowan, Dave Greenslade, John Harrison, Gary Heckstall-Smith, Jon Hiseman, Dave Lunt, Dave Moore, Colin Richardson, Christine Roche and Harry Shapiro. But most of all I am indebted to William Pryor for the unstinting help he was always ready to give, sometimes at a moment's notice. I would like to be able to say that the faults, stylistic or factual, that remain in the book are somebody else's responsibility, but they're not.
Dick Heckstall-Smith

1
Fledgling

The unconscious is that part of my history that is marked by a blank or occupied by a falsehood: it is the censored chapter. But the truth can be rediscovered; usually it had already been written down elsewhere.

Jacques Lacan, *Ecrits*

I guess I hit town as the most unfledged fledgling ever.

Nineteen fifty-six! Over thirty years ago as I sit herè. I was twenty-two, a college kid with the most tenuous of interests outside music, and pretty tightly focused music at that. Jazz, that was what got me.

But the focus was shifting fast. At fifteen, while I was at Foxhole School at Dartington, Sidney Bechet had been my musical mother, the womb in which I first took shape; at university I'd spent the summer of 1955 absorbing Lester Young in great splurging draughts. Very soon after that I'd fallen for that divine visitation in the form of a bridge between Lester and Bird: Wardell Gray – my musical father, so to speak. So when I arrived in London I was already in a state of transition, heading for bebop. What was holding me back was a combination of two things: a lack of sufficient money to buy a tenor; and the incomplete change-around in mental furniture

1

by which bebop chords become a second-nature tool of music making.

A change like that doesn't happen by accident; you have to work at it. It's a bit like the difference between arithmetic and vector analysis. A tradder learning to use bebop harmonic movements is like someone who thinks that maths is about numbers trying to understand that the really useful part of maths isn't about numbers at all, but the bits in between, the operators; you have to fight off patterns that go very deep indeed. You have to change your head, then keep it changed by constant practice until another shape of things descends on you. And that's only stage one: until you can do it intuitively you can't really do it at all – you're a two-legged avian without feathers.

I didn't become a professional overnight; I slid into it over the course of a year. People kept offering me gigs; and then one day I awoke without much surprise to the fact that I wasn't earning anything off anything else, so logically I must be a professional.

I'd left Cambridge with an awful degree in a subject which didn't interest me. I'd been heavily involved in the University Jazz Club – about the only thing I was heavily involved in – getting a silver cup, no less, for playing a good solo at the Inter-University Jazz Contest in 1955. The panel of judges that put about that silver cup was headed by Sandy Brown, the much-revered clarinettist who, two years later, gave me my first job in a band. During my last year at Cambridge there was third-hand talk of Ken Colyer maybe asking me to join his band, but this was something which didn't happen.

These were still the days of National Service, and mine had been postponed for my three university years: the nearest thing I made to a political decision in those days was to register as a conscientious objector in my last year at school. In the tribunal I had pleaded my case as a schoolboy pacifist, and been rewarded with eighteen months' hospital work instead of eighteen months' gaol. So when I came out of university, bingo! There I was, portering in the

X-ray department of St Bartholomew's Hospital, Smithfield.

After five months, I left Bart's under something of a cloud, due to the imbecile nature of the British version of the class system. By 'going out with' a young lady from Surgery I managed to cross two barriers at the same time – one up, one down. Porters were 'lower' than Surgery people, so in terms of our occupations our association was irregular and frowned upon. On the other hand, Oxbridge graduates, especially ones with hyphenated surnames, were 'higher' than young ladies from Surgery, so again our association was irregular and frowned upon. I remember being taken aside by a certain Miss W., who conceived it to be her duty to look after the moral welfare of us wide-eyed innocent young conscientious objectors in the X-ray department. She told me that So-and-So was an Awfully Nice Girl really, and she was sure she didn't have Designs on me; but all the same perhaps I ought to consider my mother's feelings in the matter and perhaps it would be better if I were to think about finding a Nice Girl from My Own Station in Life. I could scarcely credit the cheek of it! Jesus, was I pissed off.

Altogether, I was more trouble than I was worth, a disruptive influence. And, worse than that, I didn't give a damn, *and* I strongly disliked having my private life interfered with. So, I had what the authorities considered to be disgrace heaped upon me. First, I was taken out of the X-ray department and put in the General Porters' Mess. Big deal! The workload in the Mess was about a quarter of what it was in X-ray. Result: I looked far too happy to be a true penitent. Next, I was hauled up before Mr Boxall the Head Porter, in his dark-blue uniform and shiny buttons, and given a lengthy pep talk. But again – no effect. So, when it turned out that I was still 'going out with' my friend from Surgery, I was 'demoted' further: this time to the rank of cleaner. The other cleaners were fine, and the work was a piece of piss anyway, so this too was a blessing in disguise.

I continued – enthusiastically – to 'go out with' my nice young lady. She was so outraged at the way I was being treated that it made her all the keener; while the cleaners made it clear that they felt a nice young fellow like me shouldn't have to work with the likes of them, and supported me every step of the way.

Eventually I was called to see Mr Boxall again. He told me outright what a disgrace I was; that bypassed me too. Poor Mr Boxall! At his wits' end, and doubtless under some pressure from above, he was compelled to enforce the ultimate sanction. I was called in and given my cards. I still had a year and a bit of National Service to do, so I got a job as a stores porter in a hospital in Queen Square, just around the corner from where I was living. This lasted until three months later, when I got the mother and father of slipped discs from carrying too many hundredweight sacks of sugar around; it was the same nice, sexy lady from Surgery who took care of me when it happened. A certificate from the Ministry of Health went to the Ministry of Labour, and my National Service was terminated in early summer, 1957. It was then that I discovered I was a professional musician.

That summer I had to vacate the crowded flat in which I had been staying in Coburg Mansions, Handel Street, and I found myself a useful niche with three other musicians at 316 Old Brompton Road, opposite the cemetery where, with perfect irrelevance, we were told Richard Tauber was supposed to be buried.

That flat, oh boy. The others were John Mumford – still one of the best trombone players around; Colin Purbrook, whose exquisite jazz piano playing as an organ scholar at Cambridge had got him out of there before his time; and Colin Bates, who was the piano player with Terry Lightfoot. Let me tell you, it was gorgeous. We each had our own room, for a start, which was a luxury. Our landlord, Ernest Bosley, owned and ran the store on the ground floor. But although he was on the premises he was a real sweetie, a gentle, civil man who never bothered us from one year to the next as long as the rent came in on time.

There were memorable events in that flat. Talk about bachelor existence. I don't think anything got cleaned, ever. For example, after I'd been there a year or so, and long before

Mrs Bosley came upstairs for the first time, called us animals, and kicked us out in very short order (the only course of action open to a right-minded citizen), I was sitting in the kitchen having a cup of tea when a thought occurred to me. Surely, I ruminated, staring peacefully at the floor, that was green once, wasn't it? Hm! Green? Was it really? How peculiar. It certainly wasn't anything like green now; it was black. Was my memory playing tricks on me? I examined the evidence. It wasn't the angle of the light. I hadn't gone colour blind. The next time I stood up (the carsey was an original cast by the immortal Thomas Crapper of Fulham, Maker of Carseys by Appointment to Her Britannic Majesty Queen Victoria, probably worth a fortune by now), I grabbed a knife on the way back and began to investigate.

It was a hardened, flinty surface, a bit like asphalt but curiously layered, like slate. I chipped off a bit and slid the blade in and under. Whatever it was was about a quarter of an inch thick and very hard. I hammered the knife in further until about a third of the blade was under the slate stuff, then yanked it up carefully. There was a crack as the stuff split into pieces, and there before me was, yes! green lino. The slaty stuff was solidified dirt, layered and compressed by eight thoughtless male shoes every day since we'd moved in.

I was more than intrigued, I was fascinated. There was no one else about at the time, so I got going on it alone. By the time someone came in (it was tall, softly-spoken Colin Bates, the Welsh pianist from – where else? Lowestoft), I had laid bare about a quarter of the green lino. Fired with enthusiasm and the pure, holy zest for knowledge, he and I chipped away with our table knives until the whole bloody year's dirt was a pile of cracked slate in a corner by the window, and the floor was green. We showed the others when they came in. They were impressed.

In that flat we had one unbreakable rule: everyone did their own 'cooking'. To put it another way, nobody interfered with anyone else's food. Well, a lidded saucepan had stood in the same position at the back of the stove for a very long time. Nobody could remember who had last cooked with it, so nobody had interfered with it. But now, consumed (if that's

IT WAS EARLY ONE MORNING, I BELIEVE I'LL DUST MY BROOM...
...JUST TAKING THE DISHES ROUND TO THE LAUNDERETTE, DICK.
WASHING UP ROTA
CORN FLAKES
GREAT! I'LL CLEAN THE STOVE NEXT YEAR!

the right word) with investigative frenzy after our staggering floor adventure, we lifted the lid and had a look. Interested parties all of us, each with the free-thinker's eye for the unusual, we stood around and discussed it, coming eventually to the tentative conclusion that it might have been a stew at one time. Some of the bulky shapes that stirred in the body of it could once have been potatoes.

We were awed. There was a subdued but serious debate as to the possible course of action. The consensus was that to behave as if we had not seen what we had seen would be inappropriate; that it was, not to put too fine a point on it, possibly a danger to shipping. A natural culture as rudely exposed as the one we had just disrupted might strike back; it might reach criticality with disconcerting suddenness, perhaps in the middle of the night. But at the same time we were unanimous in feeling a certain debt to the gravity of the occasion, a respect for the silent majesty of this unthinkable potful! Its demise should, we agreed with solemnity, be secured by means of some uniquely memorable ceremony. We racked our brains. During these deliberations, one of us visited Mr Crapper's clinic on the landing, and found waiting sedately in its bowl a fine and shapely Richard. The answer!

Yes, that was what we did. We boiled the lot up together: ex-stew, dirt-slate from the floor, and our excellent Richard, all in one infernal brew. We took it far away. And far away was where we left it, believe me. Musicians!

Some time that autumn I was walking down the steps of the Piccadilly tube station, carrying my horn to some gig or other, when I locked eyes with a beautiful brown-haired serious-faced girl who was coming up the other side with a bloke. For some reason I remembered her.

Just before Christmas '57 I got a phone call at the flat. The phone was in the long-suffering Mr Bosley's back room downstairs behind the shop, and I remember standing there among the cardboard boxes listening to Sandy Brown (the guy who had fixed me up with that silver cup in 1955) saying, 'Wid ye like tae join ma buahnd? Ye'll be playin' taynorr.'

Shock. '*Yes*,' I shrieked carefully, anxious not to disturb Mr Bosley's customer relations. 'But I haven't got a tenor.'

'Dinna wurry aboot thaht!' said Sandy, all gruff joviality.

I didn't, and in a couple of weeks I was in the 100 Club (then the Humphrey Lyttelton Club), playing tenor with the Sandy Brown Jazzmen. It was a pretty smart group, with Derek Hogg on drums and Harry Smith on piano, besides – occasionally – Al Fairweather sitting in on trumpet.

That spring, during a gig at the 100 Club, I spied in the audience the girl I'd seen in the Piccadilly tube entrance. She was with a bloke who didn't seem to be having that much of a good time dancing with her. I didn't speak to her.

The gigs with Sandy weren't the only thing I was doing. John Mumford and I also ran a nameless but much more bebop-oriented pick-up group which we tried to fit into as many places as possible. One of them was a curious, dimly-lit basement in Gerrard Place which had thick pillars all over the room supporting the roof. There were usually about a dozen people in the audience. One night I noticed that the girl was there again, wide-eyed and serious-faced as ever, and, for heaven's sakes, blokeless! Just before the end of the set a friend of mine, Nick Whelan – he was one of the people I'd stayed with in Handel Street – went over and engaged her in conversation. Curses. Come the end of the set I whizzed off the stand. Fortunately Nick was in the Gents. 'Haven't I seen you before?' I said shamelessly – no time for niceties. I listed the sightings, anxious to wipe out any impression that I couldn't think of anything else to say. It was all very serious. By the time Nick came back I had fixed up to see her to the bus stop afterwards, exchanged phone numbers, and so on. Her name was Gary, and she was Austrian, an *au pair* girl in Swiss Cottage.

The work with Sandy continued on an even keel, through the spring of '58 – two, three, sometimes even four gigs a week. People were beginning to hear of me. But somewhere inside I wasn't satisfied. The music was fine – beautiful, smooth, classic – especially Sandy's, but it wasn't *rigorous* enough for me. I knew what was wrong: what was wrong was that it wasn't bebop.

For those days it had a great balance of styles. Sandy's band steered a serene middle course, but I didn't, and still don't, like middle courses, except as a halfway point in some transition.

I knew there were hard, tense, jagged bebop chord sequences that were there to be played within the pretty tunes we improvised on, but nobody was playing them, least of all me! Others might be not playing them by choice, but *I* wasn't playing them because I didn't know what they were. It wasn't good enough.

The following spring I got a phone call from a bloke called Ronnie Smith. Could I audition with his group? He was hoping to get an eighteen-week season in a Butlin's Holiday Camp – small-group work. I'd be the only horn player; there'd be plenty of space for solos. He hoped to make it as lively and jazzy as possible; just a sprinkling of the rock'n'rollier top twenty to keep the punters at bay.

I went and blew with them at Ronnie's mum's place in Kensal Rise: Ronnie on piano, Chuck Smith (no relation) on drums, Vernon Bown on bass, Eddie Fosh on guitar. It was fine. A cheerful team, all good players. I said yes – it would harden me up. I broke the news to Sandy at our next gig. He took it in good part, and wished me luck. It's a pity that particular Sandy Brown quintet never recorded; there are nothing but memories to tell us how it sounded.

So I spent the summer living in a sort of animal's annexe in the Southcliffe Hotel at Filey. It was an unforgettable eighteen weeks. Anything they tell you about Butlin's is likely to be true! But unfortunately anything *I* tell you is likely to be (a) lascivious and (b) libellous. Maybe I'll publish it under another name.

Gary and I got married on 15 September 1958, straight after the Filey season. After the wedding reception in Devon, at my parents' house near Totnes, we had one night's honeymoon in the incredibly noisy Railway Hotel in Bristol, then back into the maelstrom: I had a gig the next day. Any normal person would have cancelled this engagement. But a freelance jazzer? Cancel a gig?

We went to live in a basement in Ladbroke Grove – 47E Elgin Crescent. The owner of the flat was a lady of slightly

advancing years who, having been on The Stage at one time, made it clear that she understood the ways of 'showbiz people', and didn't at all mind the unusual hours we sometimes kept.

Newlyweds always have a great need to establish their own home base, I suppose, and the need is particularly strong when you're living in someone else's place. What with one thing and another, we kept ourselves to ourselves quite a lot. Our landlady seemed to have found a way of keeping herself company anyway: inside her own genteel head there was an endless supply of agreeable companions, all of whom were only too glad to use her vocal equipment. We heard lengthy conversations being conducted in animated undertones; it all seemed very convivial, seeing that there was only one person there. Once, the quorum evidently having met and come to a consensus, she approached me tactfully with: 'I think your wife's frightfully nice, Mr Heckstall-Smith, but why did you have to marry a German?' Well, it was one against many; my reply didn't get much of a hearing. I explained that I'd married my wife because I loved her, and that she was not German but Austrian, and now she was British anyway. None of that cut much ice, and in fairly short order my interlocutor(s) retired, giving a stirringly patriotic recitative about our boys having lost their lives to put a stop to this kind of thing. Gary and I left shortly afterwards. On the issue of patriotism, the fifty-four-year-old I now am thinks pretty much as I did then, that racially and nationally prejudiced beliefs are an appallingly deep-rooted, long-established and serious disease of our ex-imperialist culture. Anybody who is a real patriot struggles to uproot such things. Using that criterion, I am a real patriot.

2
Substances

Some time in 1957, before I became complete anathema to the
tradders and the New Orleans lot, Bob Wallis asked me to
guest on a record – on soprano, of course. I said yes. I always
did like Bob's New Orleans trumpet playing; to hell with
styles! One Sunday afternoon I turned up to rehearse at Studio
51 – the Ken Colyer Club in Great Newport Street as was. We
played 'Otchi Tchornya'. On drums was a flame-haired gangly
young git with blue eyes who played with the verve of a
disciplined wild animal.

Though I remember the rehearsal well, I don't remember the
session at all; in fact it wasn't until Dave Lunt, a friend of mine
who goes in for curiosities of that kind, sent me a tape of it a
couple of years back, that I realized there actually had been
such a thing. There it was: Bob Wallis's band with this soprano
player who played exactly like Sidney Bechet but wasn't
Sidney Bechet. It was only then that it dawned on me who the
drummer was – Peter Baker. That was when I first met Ginger.
How the hell we got on then, and much of what we did
together over the next three years or so, have departed from
my memory, but I do know that by 1961 Ginger and I were
doing three or four gigs together every week.

Among those gigs were the Cafe des Artistes in Redcliffe
Gardens on Thursday nights, and Rik Gunnell's All-Niters at

the Flamingo, Wardour Street, on Friday and Saturday nights. We played with the Johnny Burch Quartet, filling in between sets of Georgie Fame and the Blue Flames to packed houses of USAAF blacks. John was, and still is, one of the better jazz piano players around. (Apart from forming the Johnny Burch Octet, a trail-blazing band of the early sixties, he wrote many excellent songs, the George Fame hit 'Yeah Yeah' among them.)

I also blew a good deal in modernists' blowing haunts like the Nucleus in Monmouth Street and the Troubadour in Old Brompton Road. The Nucleus was a coffee bar with a thriving jazz basement, a place where people would come creeping in – morose, subversive, in-group, overcoat-collar-turned-up exiles carrying strange-shaped boxes – who would mumble and avert their eyes until, masonically, they came across a fellow-outcast with whom to exchange incomprehensible mutterings and cynical half-looks. I was one of them.

One scene I remember very well was Ginger and me sitting in an all-night Wimpy at St Giles's Circus after a Friday All-Niter, waiting for the first tubes to run. We were too tired for conversation, and anyway, Ginger had just 'come off' heroin and was going through shit. (He used to do that sometimes as a trial of strength. Very character-building; no doubt the Duke of Edinburgh would have approved.) After fifteen minutes of motionless silence, Ginger looked at me, mournful and red-eyed: one of the saddest and most miserable sights I have ever seen. 'Dick,' he said, 'it's like losing a friend.' What can you say to that? My heart went out to the guy. By then Ginger was a junky, and continued to be, on and off, until a few years ago, when death threatened to intervene.

Not that I was any kind of angel. I was on the pharmaceuticals too, though for me it wasn't smack and cocaine. I was using amphetamines and alcohol; and the most important, by far, was alcohol. A few words about how and why I started.

All the way through the first couple of years of being a pro I hadn't drunk anything nor felt any need to, despite being among practised drinkers – I don't seem to be particularly susceptible to social pressures, a main cause of addiction for some people, so we're told.

I didn't drink, but I was broke. Part of being a 'professional' in those days (these ones too) was having no goddamn money, so I had to go and earn a bit somewhere else. I got myself a job in Doug Dobell's jazz record shop in Charing Cross Road. As a salesman I was *terrible*! The reason: I was virtually asleep most of the time, having been up all night blowing at the Nucleus. I soon discovered that three hours' sleep between the shop closing and the Nucleus opening wasn't enough. So I invested in some little bluish-white triangular pills with rounded corners called Preludin. They were supposed to be slimming pills, to make people feel all right without eating. What they did to me was zap the hell out of me without interfering with my appetite at all.

They were amphetamines, and they were magnificent. They kept me bright and bushy-tailed, apparently without any need for sleep for quite long periods! I could earn my Dobell's pittance *and* blow my bebop changes. Once I had a spate of nearly eighty hours on the trot before my head finally found the pillow. That day-and-night Preludin routine lasted until Dobell's gave me the old heave-ho for inefficiency, the point being that I wasn't taking the Prels to stay awake in the daytime – I was taking them to stay awake at night. Bebop was the priority. I took up starving and sleeping again, but it wasn't as bad as before. I was doing more gigs by now, and I'd got some kind of a grip on bebop. I was having a good time with it.

Drugs could have some disastrous consequences for young musicians. Once, in 1961 I think it was, I played a long naughty night blowing in various parties and clubs with a mate of mine, Glen Hughes, from Georgie Fame's Blue Flames and the Johnny Burch Quartet; Glen was, in my opinion, one of the best baritone players the world has seen. A couple of years later, in bed and drugged unconscious with smack, he nodded himself to death with a cigarette in his hand. He was twenty. And please don't think that the brevity of this mention implies any light-heartedness. On the contrary. The scale of the tragedy and others like it is almost beyond words.

Glen and I had linked up with a young bass player, Pete Flick, who had an A35 van he shifted round London in. Pete was using 'blues', so called because of their colour – they were half amphetamine and half barbiturate. In the small hours of one morning we were heading north through Camden en route for Chalk Farm, Glen and I in the back and Pete's bass in the passenger seat. Suddenly there was an almighty crunch and, in no time, the police. We'd run straight into a concrete post at the side of Hampstead Road. After three days of solid 'blues', Pete had gone to sleep at the wheel, writing off his van and his bass. It was sheer luck that Glen and I were in the back, or one of us would have had no legs.

As the months passed into years, I found I had the feeling of there being something wrong. You can't make good music if

you're not carried away, and I wasn't being carried away. One night, at the pub round the corner from the Cafe des Artistes, someone said, 'Ah! Come on, have a whisky, why don't you?' So I had a quick double before I went on, and felt *great!* I was very much in charge, very aware of everything that was going on. I got carried away *and* remained in charge – the same thing really, I realized as I watched myself at it.

The alcohol was a much more significant part of the being-in-control-and-getting-carried-away-with-it bit than pills. Being in control is a lot to do with being relaxed. Alcohol enabled me to concentrate on the music, and not be distracted by other things going on in the room, or wayward thought processes. Sometimes you feel out of touch, sluggish in your reactions, as if your normal responses aren't working properly – if you were a gunfighter you'd be dead! And not because he's Jesse James either; just because you can't seem to get it together. That feeling of being out of touch is anathema to the jazzer, for obvious reasons. One thing that gets rid of that sluggish feeling is the adrenalin the body produces, the chemical shape of fear; which is why stage fright can be so productive. Having a drug aboard, unless it's totally disabling, produces effects that are rather like fear but without the unpleasant connotations. That goes for alcohol just as much as any other drugs. They all zap you, one way or another. If you can't zap yourself, they're useful.

Over the months I gradually went from one double to two doubles to three doubles to, well, quite a lot, plus of course beer. Eventually it became obvious that it would be cheaper and more reliable to buy in bulk, so I did. My own bottle. My capacity was going up fast, very fast. I was doing more work too, which meant I had to drink more. Note the 'had to'.

Alcohol's a funny thing. It can make you zappy in an instinctive sort of way like nobody's business. Then, above a certain level, it begins to slow you down again. I was getting to the stage where the amount I needed to get me to the right level was very nearly enough to begin to slow me down again. There was a margin of safety that got finer and finer; a sort of catwalk that got increasingly narrow as time went on. I needed something to widen my catwalk – something to speed me up again. It obviously wasn't more alcohol. It had to be 'yellows', amphetamine sulphate – what later became known as 'speed'. 'Blues', *à la* Pete Flick, had barbiturate in them, which I didn't need. So I eased into a routine of alcohol and yellows.

Alcohol is a total world, and by then it was my world. The yellows were just to make sure I didn't slow down any. And well, what can you say? – the results were perfectly splendid. That feeling that your body is a smoothly functioning, relatively insignificant physical appendage which enables you to do exactly what you want to do. Being stoned is being ahead of everything, up there watching and in control. A surgeon looking through a microscope at some very fine work he's doing. Someone controlling a tiny mechanical body (who looks like you) from a huge distance with the aid of an advanced total surveillance system. A long way off, but in control.

You know the normal effect of being drunk? You become less and less aware, and end up as a pathetic, snivelling, ranting, grovelling pile of flesh, less than human. Nobody can really respect anything you have to say until you are sober again. Well, apparently that doesn't happen to me, provided I'm in practice. I have a strong head, and nobody seems to know whether I'm drunk or not. But it can be dangerous. If I've got speed aboard, the difference between the right amount of alcohol and too much is obscured. Let me explain.

As far as you can tell you're behaving normally – you're in command of all your senses, you can see, understand, think, imagine, talk. Yet something funny is happening to your extremities. Your fingers won't perform the fine details of their activities properly, or if you were to vault over a row of seats you might not make it, even though under normal circumstances you wouldn't think twice.

I suppose that what's happening is this. In the millions upon millions of calculations your brain normally makes every second of the day to do with physical activity, it simply takes for granted certain basic data about your body and its surroundings. When you're pissed, that information changes, and that's you on your face. The time this basic truth really dawned on me was once in the Flamingo when I suddenly realized I couldn't play stuff I'd been playing without any difficulty three hours, two hours, even one hour ago. My head was there all right, but my fingers weren't. I stood in astonishment for a moment or two, then switched to progressively easier and easier stuff until I found my level.

That experience was a useful benchmark. After that I knew how far to go. When you really have drunk too much for muscular control to be maintained, there's only one cure – time. No amount of speed will help you out.

The diminishing returns of speed came much later, when I'd been on this regime for a good five years. It came the day after a splenetic, festering Graham Bond gig, where the music had no doubt been as marvellous as it always was. I woke up at home, 20 Barnsbury Street, and immediately realized that something very odd was going on.

Imagine that the contents of your field of vision are actually a film, being projected on to a cinema screen, and 'you' are sitting in the auditorium watching it. Now imagine that the projectionist suddenly switches on a second projector, one showing a completely different film, so that both films are being projected on to the same screen. That is what I opened my eyes to the next day – two 'films' going on in front of my eyes at the same time, one of them real life and the other not, both perfectly realistic and ordinary-looking. There was no immediate way of telling which was the real one except by the use of logic and memory. Neither was at all nightmarish; the only nightmarish part was that there were two of them.

That was a bit of a shaker. I didn't go on about it too much, but I knocked those yellows on the head forthwith, and even cut down on the Teacher's a bit. I suppose I was slightly gratified that nobody else seemed to notice any difference.

Looking back on it, I don't think that my stimulant period had all that much to do with music, except in the essentially marginal way that when I first started using it, it administered a kind of mental jerk that kicked me a long way in a short time. When I stopped, though, I noticed that I hadn't progressed much, and I'd been repeating myself a lot.

As a drinker, I've never wanted to try heroin or cocaine, so I

make no claim to know what it's all about from the inside. But I have wondered. A couple of people have done their very creditable best to wise me up, including my father. His autobiography, *Doubtful Schoolmaster*, mentions his experience of morphia during the First World War:

Being wounded in the summer of 1917 was a queer experience. My battery was two miles south of Ypres, and we had been having rather a thick night as the targets of what was known as neutralizing fire – fire designed not to destroy a battery but to keep it inactive. At about noon the next day the conscientious Germans broke off for lunch, and we thought we might have lunch too – the best we could get. The sherry, the whisky and the port left me with my usually well-developed senses of fear and caution atrophied, and as I stumped home – I had got water on the knee playing hide-and-seek round the guns in moonlight the night before, and my left leg was stiff and bandaged – to the windmill I was billeted in, the shelling began again. I sat down in a shell-hole to avoid splinters, and then felt for the first and last time in my life that it was silly to take any notice of desultory harassing fire. I got up and walked on. The next round fell behind me, and I felt a heavy thump on the calf of my right leg. It did not hurt at all, and I ran all out to the far side of a haystack just beyond the road from Ypres to Armentières. I flopped behind this haystack and immediately noticed a thick stream, about as thick as my middle finger, coming out in jets at right angles to the leg for several inches. Instantly I felt a surge of joy so intense that it is still almost always near the surface of my mind, ready to reappear. I thought:

(1) This is the perfect wound, no doubt about it – no permanent damage, and it doesn't hurt.

(2) This makes me one of the ordinary people of all history who have been knocked out in a war. Dr Johnson said, 'Every man thinks meanly of himself if he has not been a soldier.'

(3) If I don't do something quickly I shall bleed to death in five minutes and *waste* it.

I unwound the very opportune bandage from my left knee and pulled it tight around my right calf, using a handy bit of stick as a tourniquet. I stopped the bleeding, and was delighted to find that already I could not get up. There was lots of blood about, and it deeply impressed a man of my battery who happened to pass, but not two infantrymen who saw me from the road. They warmly and unreservedly congratulated me, carried me to a passing truck, and gave me a cigarette so I could complete the picture of the nonchalant wounded hero. Once was enough, but oh to have done it once! How ordinary and how delightful! I lay for some hours on a stretcher in the entrance hall of the hospital at Bailleul. The blood was still impressive and a sympathetic nurse whispered, 'Would you like some morphia?' I was in no pain, I knew I was all right, and objected on principle to drugs for fun, but thought this was the one legitimate chance of a lifetime. 'Yes,' I whispered.

And almost immediately there swept over me an even more profound bliss. I was put under at 1 a.m. for the operation . . . and I woke for a minute at 8 a.m. feeling not so good.

Well, I was interested in that 'even more profound bliss', so when the chance next came round I asked him what it meant. I chose my moment – it was while we were walking back over the hill from a pub lunch in Harberton, a village three or four miles from his home in Devon. He was seventy by then, and a diabetic, so we were walking pretty slowly up the hill. He stopped. Stroking his chin contemplatively, he stood thinking for a minute or two, staring over the hedge. Then he said: 'Suppose you had a farm which was just small enough for you to run on your own, and it was harvest time, so you had to work every daylight hour in the fields. Now, suppose it's the end of the day, and you've come home exhausted, eaten your dinner, and gone up to your bedroom longing for your bed. You undress and put on your pyjamas; you pull back the bedclothes and get in; then you pull the bedclothes up to your chin. *That's* the moment. It's like that,' he said, 'only it's all the time.'

I once asked Ginger what it was like, too, just to check. Same kind of thing. He stopped and thought, too, just like my dad. Then he said, 'It's just like the moment you come. Except that it goes on. It doesn't stop.'

Make what you like of that. It's enough for me. Whatever smack is like, it clearly isn't like alcohol. The physical delight that's obviously such a big part of it isn't anything to do with drink. The alcohol/speed thing did not directly affect my physical experiences – it just gave me a sense of *ability*. People have told me that sounds like cocaine. I wouldn't know.

In those Johnny Burch Quartet Flamingo All-Niters I used to do with Ginger, John Gunnell (Rik's younger brother – his voice is the one you hear going on about Cokes if you listen to Georgie Fame's *Live at the Flamingo* album) used to fill in the changeovers. It was always the same record – a Ray Charles collection, with 'I Can't Stop Loving You' at the top.

At the time I was switching back from gin to whisky, plus experimenting with 140-proof Vyborova, plus of course the yellows, and while getting out my horn and warming up, fixing a Coke-bottle-ful of Teacher's, talking, etc, that Ray Charles's music just came shooting through. I couldn't help noticing it.

For me some music – parts of the B Minor Mass for example, and much of Purcell – completely beggars words like 'emotional' and 'tragic'. Dignified and intense, it's the rich, full, perfect distillation of a state for which there is no name. It is music from which has been removed all trace of the sentimental – all trace, indeed, of anything comfortingly human. It seemed to me that Ray Charles's performance of that particular number was of a piece with such music. The absolute ground-zero loss that it spoke of – loss without complications, without impurities, without the slightest edge of bitterness or anger, without any slop or slush – could not possibly (despite the title) come from an attachment to a human being. Attachments to human beings are just not like that! There's always a life-giving little residue of anger at the end of a friendship or a love relationship, just because the person was human. But what

Ray Charles was singing about was not in that world at all: there was no two-waying in it, just utter hopelessness lifted to the level of great music, without a shred of anger or conflict. Nothing for the wounded ego to latch on to and begin to repair itself with. It had to be something else he was singing about.

Well, I thought, I think *I* know what it is, even if no one else does. It's heroin that he's singing about. And that chimed in with the feeling I'd had when Ginger talked about 'losing a friend', it explained why it would have been utterly pointless to tell him that he hadn't lost *my* friendship (he assumed that anyway; we both did). The bottom line was that it *wasn't* like losing a friend! On the contrary, the good thing about friends and lovers is that they're *not* you, and the bad thing about heroin is that in the end it *is* you. So went my thoughts as I puzzled it all out, my conclusions appearing like a precipitate out of a large vague cloud of vapour.

I recognized two things at the same time: the sincerity of that feeling, and the utter worthlessness of it. That's why I've never been in the slightest bit tempted by my beloved father's 'even more profound bliss' – quite the reverse. The whole thing seems such an outrage upon the human spirit, on *my* spirit, that I would never have imposed it on my own body. Put another way, there's enough of the prig in me to come down on the whole idea like a ton of bricks. Other people had their scenes; I had mine, and mine didn't include that kind of bliss. Thanks, but no.

Much later, in 1973, I had another piece of insight shoved down my throat. I was cut down by an extremely drastic case of lumbar disc collapse – back trouble. The pain was indescribable, and to begin with nothing would control it, not even morphine. Later, when I was recovering, the doctor put me on a close relation of morphine called DF118; I was on a fairly heavy DF118 regime for about eight weeks. It made life bearable.

When I was better, I was taken off it again. Instantly I found that my entire outlook had changed: all of a sudden the world was a world of tears. That was something I had never felt before. From within this new strange miserable world of tears I realized that there was nothing at all outside of me that could have caused me to feel like that. 'Objectively', as they say, everything was looking good for me – it was only from the inside that everything seemed hopeless.

At that, something inside me rose up in an ice-cold implacable fury; a rage the like of which I've scarcely imagined in my adult life. I perceived that I, Dick Heckstall-Smith, was being compelled by nothing more than the absence of some bloody chemical to feel emotions that were not mine! I have never felt such a profound animal resentment as I felt at that DF118's unforgivable intrusion on *my* bloody privacy. What cheek! A chemical dictating to me how I should feel!

Quite an experience, that.

While we're on the subject, there's someone I have to mention – that doyen of British drummers Phil Seamen, a legendary figure if ever there was one, and someone who we'll meet again briefly later. He lived with me for a couple of months in the early sixties, and he told me something that's always stayed with me, the story of how he got 'on' (hooked) in the first place.

He *decided* to, all in the space of half an hour, in the compartment of a train on the way to Manchester.

Apparently he was working very, very hard at the time – in the fifties it was – and he was on his way to do a radio show, followed by a gig with that other jazz legend, Ronnie Scott. Alone in his compartment and extremely short of sleep, he faced his problem. Up till then he'd been using heroin and cocaine, though very carefully, and he wasn't yet addicted. His physical symptoms were telling him two opposite things. If he used drugs today, he would be addicted for the rest of his (shortened) life. If he didn't use the drugs, he wouldn't be able to do justice to the gig – he would, by his standards, be a bad drummer. He had a really bad half-hour, and by the end of it he had decided. He was going to be as good a drummer as it was possible to him to be, for whatever time remained to him. He went off to the toilet with his works and shot up . . .

The clarity of this story, and the clarity of the decision, increased my respect for Phil enormously.

The years '59, '60 and '61 were ones of financial hand-to-moutherie – freelancing any- and everywhere, eager both for the pittance of a meal ticket at the end of a gig and for the chances that might come my way to blow jazz. Jazzwise I did fairly well, especially out of town – London never really took me on board, I guess.

I even made a few records as a sideman around those years, though I'd be hard put to it to say which now.

Workwise, though, there were some stints with names. There was the infamous and excellent Basil Kirchin Small Band – a season in Romano's, a shortlived nightclub in Gerrard Street. That band was a dynamic little combo if ever there was one: it must have surprised a few nightclub-goers! There was Basil's lumpy, gutsy sidekick Ashley Kozak on bass; Tony Dakis, the Welsh Greek wizard of the jazz accordion; and Johnny Beard on alto. An education, that. One of the most powerful images I have (and I still use it sometimes when teaching) is of what happened when John's horn came apart just as he had to blow 'Autumn Leaves' in some godforsaken slow foxtrot medley.

I'd done my bit by then – I was probably lighting a Capstan Full Strength under the music stand or something – anyway, I wasn't paying too much attention. John leaned across and said in his guttural cannabis-and-Red-Barrel-laden tones, 'Me alto's fucked, take it will yer?'

'What key?' I asked, realizing there was only a bar of Tony's tiny key-change left, to which Johnny swiftly said, 'I dunno, but it starts *here*,' showing me his fingers on the alto in the position for an E.

Not only did he not know what key it was, he didn't even know the names of the notes! And yet he read faultlessly, and his jazz was perfect, classical bebop, Mozart-like in its delicacy, bla bla bla – I mean it too. John played exquisitely. Thinking about it afterwards, of course, I realized that it makes sense. If your ear's *that* good, you don't need to know any of those things. When you actually get down to it, music is neither knowledge nor marks on paper, but sounds; instruments are machines which, if manipulated rightly, will make those sounds.

There was a somewhat extraordinary five-month-long tour playing baritone in the pit of the Jerome Robbins Ballet USA. Three British saxophone players were employed to give life to a post-*West Side Story* jazz scene by Bernstein; we were working under a real flesh-and-blood conductor, Werner Torkanowsky. Covering the whole of Europe from Lisbon to Reykjavik to Warsaw, and including Israel, that tour used up the entire summer of 1959. I played Tel Aviv with a temperature of 104°, having got typhus from swimming in the tideless, torpid, shit-filled Mediterranean . . . *and* I very very nearly got my head chopped clean off by the propeller of a speedboat in the Adriatic off Dubrovnik.

After that there was another nightclub gig, the Blue Lagoon. It made my embouchure like iron; at five hours a night, six nights a week, it couldn't fail. In 1960 I got some more regular London gigs, including the Cafe des Artistes and the Flamingo All-Niters. That was when one of the most hard-wearing friendships of my life began – that with Eddie Jackson of Chicago.

One night I was playing the Cafe. After I came off, a pair of obviously American blacks came up to me. The shorter, blacker one introduced himself as Ronnie; his larger, lighter-skinned, unsmiling companion was Eddie. The conversation was jazz, jazz, jazz – they were both from Chicago, and were full of how good it was to hear real music over here. They came back the next week, and we spoke again. Over the months, Eddie and I gradually came to exchange deeper views. I found that we could communicate. I liked his quietness, his apparently impenetrable solemnity, his deeply concealed acid sense of humour, the fact that he took things seriously. He must have found something attractive in me as well, because two and a half decades later we're still in contact with each other.

Eddie was over with the USAAF – it was through his subtle clandestinerie that I ended up sleeping inside Wethersfield. Don't think I'd do that now.

Autumn 1961 saw me doing a month in West Germany with a sextet run by a very fine British trumpet player, Bert Courtley – all with Ginger Baker. Ginger and I were doing quite a bit of playing together around that time; as much as we could organize, anyway. We were forever moaning on about the flabbiness and introverted anti-audience stance of much of the London jazz scene. Back in 1960 I'd done some gigs with a band led by a Canadian trumpet player called Dick Williams, who later became *the* Richard Williams, the animator who invented the Pink Panther. As a result I'd managed to get a night under my own name at the Cafe des Artistes, on which I promptly booked Ginger. It was around then that something happened which has left another of those irrelevant but powerful little memories which for some reason never let go.

Ginger and I are on a late bus with our instruments, going home after a late one at the Cafe (just imagine it: a full-time pro gig drummer taking his drums home on a bus! But it was all too normal – nobody in our scene could possibly have afforded a car.) It's one o'clock in the morning; there's no traffic about, and the bus, empty but for us and a couple of other people, is careering happily round Hyde Park Corner. As it heads up Park Lane there's a series of monster crashing sounds which seem to disappear progressively behind us. Ginger looks out of the back of the top deck where we're sitting, and lets out a great warbling shriek of furious anger. It's his drums! There they are, all bits and pieces spread out over the shiny asphalt. The little below-stairs LT luggage compartment has failed to hold them. The bus shudders to a frightened halt, and Ginger, long-legged and short-tempered, nine stone of red-rimmed Irish Cockney, gallops off to his babies, calling down fire and brimstone on a defensive conductor. Aided by my good self, he retrieves them, and off we go again.

And another memory. A gig in Westbourne Grove, Friday 25 March 1960. It's a jazz group – a sort of Anglo-Swedish prance-up sort of thing – put together by Kris Elkington, a drummer I'd known in Cambridge. I'm blowing into the mike at the front of the stage, which is about a yard high. In the crowd in front of me is a smartly-dressed, wide young bloke with a square black crewcut – very hip in those days – and a pencil moustache. He's watching me fixedly. At the end of the set he comes up to the stage and introduces himself, so we're shaking hands and so on with a yard's difference in elevation.

His name, he says, is Graham Bond, and as he rabbits on I remember where I've seen him before: a silent humble figure with a plastic alto, a Grafton, who was always on the outskirts of the Nucleus scene, never ever part of it. He says he's really glad to see me blowing so well, and asks if he can have a blow with me, it would do him a power of good. OK, I say, ask Kris . . .

So he plays, with great verve and obvious pleasure. Afterwards he buttonholes me again. He is urgently affable, pressing, quite passionate indeed. He is more glad than he can say to hear me playing the way I am – it's an inspiration to him. He had been driven to the depths of depression by the exclusiveness of the Nucleus scene, he tells me. So much had he felt there was no place for him that he'd decided to give up the alto, give up music altogether. Until tonight! Hearing the way I am playing he feels very close to me. I've given him hope, and now he feels the strength to go on. Suddenly he feels he isn't alone.

All this he says with wide-eyed and very direct eyeball-to-eyeball engagement.

3
Blues Incorporated

Sometimes, in interviews and suchlike, I get asked why I left the jazz scene. There are hints here and there throughout the early part of this book, I think, but it's only fair that I try to say something about it directly. Now's the time.

The kind of jazz I like – the kind of *music* I like – is strong, pushy, forward, full-blooded, free of self-imposed restrictions. It takes risks. It is not in the least afraid; it battles its way through to expression. It is full of mistakes, but couldn't care a jot about them because it knows that mistakes are its life-blood. It is unashamed, it can flow like a river over the rapids or a delta over the mud. When it senses unhealthy restraint it plants a bomb under it and trips the detonator. It shows no mercy for half measures. It doesn't care about good taste. But this is not to say it can't be beautiful. Its beauty is that of strength triumphing over ugliness.

I began to feel that audiences and musicians alike had somehow got on the wrong road, had somehow been browbeaten into believing that it wasn't quite right to enjoy themselves too openly, that they should sit quietly and assess rather than have a good time. Oh, I loved jazz! But I didn't love good taste, and I began to feel that there was altogether too much good taste in the British jazz scene.

I found what I was missing in Blues Incorporated and its audiences.

One late, late evening in February 1962 I was to be found in the basement of the Troubadour in Old Brompton Road. I'd been there lots of times before: the place was one of the more popular blowing gaffs – popular, that is, among the boppers and the few scattered aficionados. The average punter would have run a mile, I guess. This particular session was distinguished by the presence, noted but not acknowledged, of a non-bopper – to wit, a blueser. It did of course occasionally happen that foreign bodies strayed into the ointment – not necessarily bluesers, just any non-bopper – and we knew from experience that the situation could normally be taken care of fairly painlessly by a quick dose of the freeze-out. People can't stand being ignored. Usually.

But this cuckoo in the nest wasn't responding. On the contrary, as number succeeded number and our mystery guest was pointedly left out of what little verbal intercourse there was – either abstruse musicians' jokes or esoteric mumblings about chord sequences and basslines – he seemed to thrive. His guitar playing was always there though, sticking out like a sore thumb.

Slim and swarthy, he was neatly dressed and of medium height, with a genial self-possessed demeanour and a smile like a cat's; a smile that spelled danger. You could almost see the healthy teeth becoming more and more pointed as he listened, ever affable, to the conversation, and played blues phrases over everything from 'Cherokee' to 'My Ship' to 'There Will Never be Another You', however dazzlingly intricate the chord sequences that bubbled underneath him – a practice that would make any self-respecting bebopper go grey with horror and cover his ears. And invariably he came up smiling, ready for the next hatchet job. He seemed set to go on like that all night.

War had been declared: Assembled Boppers *vs.* the Lone Blueser. Under cover of music making, ideological struggle – wordless as arm-wrestling, but no less intense for that – filled the little Fulham cellar. It should have been No Contest from the start, considering the sheer weight of numbers on the boppers' side, but it wasn't. The Lone Blueser was deploying a secret and lethal weapon: an armour-plated personality with such an inbuilt level of embarrassment-resistance that whatever silent brickbats and vibes came his way he remained cheerful, relaxed and unaffected.

It was an epic in its way, no quarter given or asked: the end could come only when one side or the other had left the premises. The good old Weakest Link hypothesis precipitated the outcome: first one bopper packed his horn, mumbling something about having a long way to go home and a session in the morning. Then, at shorter and shorter intervals, the remainder simply melted away. As the numbers of beboppers decreased, so did the level of ideological firepower: the blueser had an easier and easier passage as time passed. In the end he won. It was some kind of object lession.

Was it an empty victory? Was he the only soldier left standing?

No. Though I was a bopper, an ardent one with a long way to go musically and not long enough to do it in, I hadn't left. And why not? Because ever since my Devon schooldays I'd had a penchant for blues – through fellow Dartingtonians Charlie Howard, Jeremy Wiseman and Niall O'Casey I'd heard Sonny Terry and Brownie McGhee, Muddy Waters, Lonnie Johnson, Josh White, Leadbelly . . . I loved them early and dearly, and sometimes, as a saxophone-playing imitation guitarist, I liked to play them. None of the other hornmen had seemed at all blues-inclined, though. It was as if, seeing how rigidly single-minded our foreigner was, they'd followed his example and refused to learn from him either. Not so with me, however, and the two of us ended up playing blues together.

Came the death. We grinned, stood up and introduced ourselves. His name, said the suave one, was Alexis Korner. (Aha! I thought to myself, I'm not surprised you didn't introduce yourself earlier!) He was thinking of starting up a Chicago-style blues band later that year, with brass in it. He'd been looking for horn players who might be able to fit in; would I be interested? Well, freelancers always say yes on the principle that one in ten comes up and that way you might keep afloat, so I said yes. Phone numbers were exchanged and cordial goodbyes said. I went home to Archway, thinking to myself on the night bus that I'd had an interesting blow one way or another. Then I forgot all about it.

Some time in April or May I got a phone call. It was a personable upper-class voice which, oddly, I recognized straight away. Could I make a rehearsal at the Round House in Wardour Street a couple of Mondays hence? I checked the ever-present diary and said yes.

'Great, Dick. See you then, then.' He always addressed people by their names, did Alexis.

I showed up at seven on the day we'd arranged. No one there. Not unusual. I got my horn out. The drummer arrived and we introduced ourselves: 'Watts,' he said, 'Charlie Watts. But I'm not much good, I'm afraid.' The bass player arrived – Andy Hoogenboom – then Alexis, full of bonhomie, struggling with a guitar and amp, then the piano player, Keith Scott. We talked, set up, had a vague blow, got in tune. It seemed we were still waiting for someone. At ten to eight the clattery pub-room double doors were flung open and a burly balding figure in a dirty raincoat pushed in, holding an old and very bulging briefcase. Ignoring the good-natured shouts of 'Hullo, Cyril!' he made his way straight to the decrepit upright piano in the corner of the room, and upended his briefcase over the top of it. An enormous number of harmonicas flowed out, rather like a liquid, and he cursed roundly and obscenely.

That was my introduction to Cyril Davies, panel-beater, the first fully-fledged genius I ever worked with on a regular basis. I say 'fully-fledged' advisedly. Cyril had already developed to full and magnificent completion in every area of his music, slice it how you like. All his potentials were actuals, external-ized without reserve every time he played. To feel the beauty and the power, the accomplishment of *music*, that came across when Cyril performed, was almost to feel a physical force. He was so good there was no point comparing him with anybody else – that's what I mean by fully-fledged.

Cyril was angry. He was angry because there was a saxophone in the room. He disapproved, morally, of saxophones! I didn't fully understand this fact for the first couple of weeks. At first I thought it was just me he disliked, but it wasn't. I reasoned that it couldn't be that, because he and I got on well straight away, partly by being drunk together on gigs, and partly because he was a Welshman who had been brought up in England, while I was an Englishman brought up in Wales. Then I thought maybe it was my playing, but it wasn't that either. He liked my playing – he just didn't like what it was played on.

He simply could not abide saxophones at any price, and this attitude was part and parcel of an utterly and translucently pure fervour for a *style* of art. No thriving artform is without a core of devastating intolerance on the part of its producers for styles other than their own. Cyril's attitude was unchangeable, unchallengeable and impervious. He could see very clearly the difference between the producer and the product, so there was no personal animosity at all, but he could not reconcile the style he loved with any sound created by a saxophone, however well played.

So it's not surprising that Cyril had to leave in the end, thus destroying the best and most utterly dynamite Blues Inc. ever heard (in my opinion). But that wasn't to be for a while yet.

Cambridge May Balls take place – naturally! when else? – in June, and my links with Cambridge University meant that from time to time I was called up and asked to play there. The poor buggers probably didn't know anyone else, and anyway, with a goddamn hyphenated surname I must be the right sort of chap, what? Not too much of a bounder.

It was summer 1962. I'd been doing gigs since the previous autumn – as a freelance of course – with the Bert Courtley Sextet, a good solid middle-of-the-road modern-jazz unit with a good reliable book. Ginger was in it too, and that suited me. When an entertainments committee secretary from St John's College, Cambridge rang me up and asked me, a freelance tenor player, to put a gig together, I had to work hard to put together a group that would pass muster as a band, and have enough music to play three full sets.

I phoned Bert. 'Bert, I've got a gig. Can I borrow your band for the night, and will you be my trumpet player? The bread's good: it's a May Ball.'

Bert was rather tickled. The band wasn't working that night, so sure I could use the band. Why didn't I ring round everyone and check them out? He thought it was a bit much for him to masquerade as his tenor player's trumpet player – why didn't I phone Johnny Huckridge? It suited me. John was a magical trumpet player who had a tendency to nerves, and hence too much drink, when faced with the solo limelight. Perhaps in the relative obscurity of 'Dick Heckstall-Smith's Band' he'd feel free to show himself in his true light. He did.

So come the night, the band – Kathy Stobart, Johnny, Maurice Salvat on bass, Ginger and, I think, Colin Purbrook on piano – played the first set. Towards the end of it this little bloke came to the stage, and in a powerful Scottish accent asked if he could play with us.

'What do you play?' I asked.

'Ah plee be-ass,' he answered.

There are all sorts of possible responses when a total stranger asks for a sit-in. If you're a complete nutter, you can of course say yes no matter what, and end up collapsing under a plague of loonies who don't know they can't play. (It's amazing how quickly and with what Olympian confidence idiot sitters-in can hijack a perfectly good set.) Or you can simply play it thick, and always say no – the risks are a great deal less, but it's a bit, well, unadventurous. Best is to use a combination of tactics and instinct. The standard approach – unless the gig's a jam session anyway – is to make it difficult but not impossible for the sitter-in, both logistically and musically, until you've got a smell of him.

So I said, 'No, not now. It's too late.'

'Are ye playin' anither sait?' he asked.

'Well, yes.'

'Can Ah plee wi' ye thain?'

'Mmm,' I said. 'OK!'

Well, he was persistent anyway. I took pity – the second set

wasn't in the marquee, and I couldn't see the poor bugger
bringing his bloody bass all the way to the wrong place. 'It's in
the cellars somewhere,' I said. 'I don't exactly know where, but
bring your own bass, eh? Our bass player won't want to lend
you his, I don't think.'

'Oh-kee,' said the little guy, nodding grimly, and off he
went. He was about eighteen, if that.

And lo, he showed up in the cellars at half past one, visible
at first only by the top end of a string bass moving slowly
through a dense area of bobbing, shrieking hoorays. Eventually he surfaced by the stone flagging we were playing on.
Ginger and I exchanged a look. Tactic 17b was indicated.
'Hullo,' I said after we'd finished what we were playing.
'D'you want a play then?' Better get it over with.

'Aye,' he said.

Maurice stepped out for a fag and a smash at one of the
hooray girls. He was good at girls.

'Twelve-bar in beef,' I called, and counted in 'Blue 'n'
Boogie', which is normally a fastish, vaguely boppy riff; a nice,
neat, simple hook to hang long solos on, so that whether it's
bad or good depends almost entirely on how well it's played.
That night it went at an absolutely fiendish tempo. I counted it
in as fast as my fingers would move. It was so goddamn fast
that the choruses came and went before you could blink – it
must have been eight or nine choruses a minute. And holy shit
– the little guy stormed into it like there was no tomorrow,
heads down and no prisoners from the off. It was demonic. I
remember exchanging a soul-awakening, wowee-here-we-go
glance with a grinning Ginger a few bars in; after that it was
straight through the roof and devil take the hindmost. It was
glorious. It swung like the clappers.

Nobody said anything afterwards. He was much better than
Maurice. 'OK,' I said, 'we'll do "Lover Man" in F. You play the
tune. Two, three, four . . .' And by God he did! Beautifully.
Faultlessly. Vibrato, in tune, the lot. All the changes.

Of course he did. He was Jack Bruce, only I didn't know that
then. Neither did anybody else, anywhere, except I guess Jack.

He was going to London next, he said. We exchanged names
and phone numbers.

At the beginning, Alexis had only one Blues Incorporated gig a week – a thriving Sunday-night residency at the Ealing Club in Ealing Broadway. I can still recall a vivid sense of that club, made up from a great many instances which have furrowed great grooves in my cranium. One of the strongest elements in this amalgam is remembering the heat, sweat and over-crowdedness – my dad would have hated it. It seemed to be perpetually full, erupting lavalike with screeching, raving, compressed underground life – like a lot of good clubs, I guess. But it also had something that the discreet, horn-rimmed, note-taking, unsmiling jazz clubs in town lacked: enthusiasm. The beehive-barneted sixteen-year-olds and their smart red-faced loose-lipped paramours all seemed to be having a roaring good time, dancing, watching, listening. It wasn't an atmosphere where discretion attracted any attention, never mind approval!

When I got to Blues Inc., it was immediately apparent that parts of it were better than other parts. Unlike a lot of groups, it was a *band* – it had a unity and dynamic musical character of its own which transcended the individuals in it. That was rare, and it had to be nurtured. It was what made the band so good, and without it, Blues Inc. would not have held me. It was also very clear that it was Alexis, and not the nonpareil Cyril, whose influence stood behind this state of affairs – a subtle, gentle strength, at times quite subversive. Cyril was the genius, but not the leader.

I couldn't help wondering how the band would sound with Jack in it, so I asked Alexis if a friend of mine could come along and have a play.

'All right,' said Alexis, 'bring him along on Sunday.'

How exactly it came about that Andy Hoogenboom left and Jack joined I don't know, but once Jack was in, things shifted into a new gear.

For a long time now I'd been getting Ginger into any gigs I could, such as the Johnny Burch Quartet at the Flamingo. The discovery of Jack had, of course, stretched the Ginger-and-I partnership into a triumvirate whenever possible, so with Jack and I in Blues Inc., it was clearly time for Ginger to have a sit-in, and the opportunity came one Thursday night at the

Marquee (now the defunct Academy Cinema) on the corner of Poland Street and Oxford Street. Charlie Watts, who already dug Ginger's playing, was quite happy to step out for a bit, and the sit-in went on all night. What happened afterwards was extraordinary. It became clear that Charlie actually *wanted* Blues Inc. to have Ginger in it; and believe it or not, the deal was struck there and then. It was in my experience a unique way for a personnel change to take place, and a wholehearted hats-off to Charlie Watts for it. The reasoning behind Charlie's move that night was that, apart from genuinely wanting to have Ginger as the drummer, Charlie didn't want to turn professional. He thought it was too unstable and insecure a life, financially speaking. *O tempora, o mores!* He walked straight into a group that sometimes did Alexis's intervals, called the Rolling Stones.

Meanwhile things had been moving on. Keith Scott had vacated the piano chair, Dave Stevens joining in his stead. But Dave, a gloriously joyful player in the Earl Hines tradition and a chartered accountant by trade, felt that the increasing number of out-of-town gigs was putting too much of a strain on his resources. So Johnny Parker joined. And, with the advent of Ginger, *the* classic Blues Incorporated line-up, one which I think could not be bettered, was set: Alexis Korner: guitar and vocals; Cyril Davies: harp, vocals, twelve-string; Dick Heckstall-Smith: tenor sax; Johnny Parker: piano; Jack Bruce: string bass; Ginger Baker: drums.

Oddly enough, though, no recordings made by this line-up were ever issued, though it did record. It did an album in Decca's big basement studio. I have a rough-mix two-track of one number, 'Dooji Wooji', but the tapes were never mixed, and as far as I know no one ever issued any of the tracks. I can still remember recording that number – it was one o'clock in the afternoon, and I was stone-cold sober. It was great. Incidentally, the band on the so-called Blues Inc. *Live at the Marquee* album isn't the same line-up – the line-up on the album never played at the Marquee.

I started with Blues Inc. purely as a freelance; though the band was very special, sentiment can't stand in the way of making a living. It wasn't really in competition with my other gigs, as to begin with it was only doing one residency a week. When Alexis announced the second residency at the Marquee on Thursday nights, it just put me up to five regulars a week – two Blues Inc. nights on Sundays and Thursdays, the Cambridge Jazz Club on Wednesdays, and the Flamingo All-Niters at the weekend.

But the next thing I knew, the Thursdays had leapt from a dead-small day-before-payday attendance of fifty or so to four or five hundred – some even hinted eight hundred, though I remember noticing that the figure got more difficult to discover the higher it went. The band was attracting attention.

A blues band, attracting attention! And it didn't seem to be a trad spill-over crowd either. They just weren't traddy-looking people – too young, too hip. Well well! I didn't get too excited about that, but I did get excited about the music.

Then Alexis started getting out-of-town gigs. Manchester, the odd university, occasional weekends away. Clashes with previous longstanding commitments began to arise. They always do when a freelancer works with a band where the identity of the players is important. I could find deps for my regular club nights, but it wouldn't have worked with Blues Inc. – to have done so would have virtually meant giving up my place in the band. It was sometimes a problem knowing what to do. If I wanted to go on being a freelance musician I had to take all the gigs I could get, but some of those gigs – the very ones that made the freelance existence more viable – were demanding more and more that I commit myself fully to them at the expense of the other bookings.

'There comes a time,' sings Zoot Sims, 'when a man must make up his mind.' Alexis knew it; Cyril, Jack and Ginger knew it; I knew it. Alexis couldn't realistically offer a weekly wage, but he could offer a reasonably full Blues Inc. book. Politely, he requested first call on my services.

The ultimate dilemma of the freelance. As soon as you start turning down gigs, people gradually stop ringing you – not because of anything personal, just because it's more likely to be a wasted phone call. Your name drops inexorably down everyone's lists until eventually it falls off the bottom. There are always more freelancers than there is work, and the whole freelance business depends on people being *free*.

I waited to see what would happen. Blues Inc.'s workload increased; there was a clash of dates, the freelancer's nightmare. I decided to join.

At the end of November a bombshell hit. Alexis phoned to say that Cyril had decided to leave to form his own band. Could I come to a band meeting?

It was very sad. I remember a morosely formal gathering at Alexis and Bobby's flat in Moscow Road from which the usual flippant, cheerful, sideswiping humour was absent, leaving only serious feelings and the reasons behind them as subjects of discussion. Alexis and Cyril must have had it out first *in camera*: they were presenting a united front to the rest of us. Cyril sat in an armchair looking worried while Alexis explained how he saw the dilemma. Cyril, Alexis explained, felt that the band was getting too jazzy for him. While he recognized the quality of the music and didn't want to criticize the band on that score, the presence of a jazz-influenced drummer and the ominous saxophone were turning the band in a direction which, musically faultless though it was, he didn't personally want to follow. Then Cyril spoke up. Gruffly, awkwardly, seriously, he said how much he regretted the passing of his long association with Alexis, and told us of his plans to strike out on his own with a more authentically-instrumented blues line-up. Alexis wished Cyril every success with his new venture. Cyril said dutifully how good he thought everyone was. But he felt he had no choice but to go.

It was a major upheaval.

A few days later, I was walking down Shaftesbury Avenue with Alexis. He seemed quite unperturbed. Never one for dragging his feet in the mud created by spilt milk, he examined the future with quiet excitement. He felt he had two alternatives – either to find another singer and harp player, or to find another genius who could fill Cyril's Olympian shoes. In Chicago we might have found someone who could fill both requirements, but this was the London of 1962.

Alexis was convinced that it had to be a genius. If it was a choice between stylistic purity and intrinsic musical value, someone who could fill an elated audience with excitement, then it had to be the latter. So who?

'Graham Bond,' said Alexis ecstatically, breathing out cigar smoke with the smug catlike smile of the bloke in the Panatella ad. He'd already thought the whole bloody thing through – I suspect he'd already approached Graham.

Graham was an obvious choice. Whoever was to fill Cyril's place had to play a front-line instrument, and play it well – and Graham did. He played a magnificent shouting alto with glorious soul, a bluesy bebop feel, and all the natural panache of Cannonball Adderley. (Somewhat weirdly, the Graham of those days resembled Cannon physically, with his eighteen stone and his smart grey suit, black crewcut and narrow black moustache.) But what was crucial was the size and magniloquence of Graham's personality, and the fact that it expanded on stage. Superficially Graham and Cyril had very little in common, but underneath, where it mattered, Graham was born to do what Cyril had done in that fathomlessly delicate matter of band–audience dynamics. Graham could carry the job.

With twenty-seven years' hindsight, I can see now that Graham coincided with Alexis's plans in another way. He wanted to move on, fast. Using the blues-band image as a sort of cover, Alexis wanted to slide into having a band playing good music to a big enthusiastic audience. A band with a common touch, but playing wonderful crypto-avant-garde-ish Mingus-influenced blues music. Cyril may have been right all along about those jazz influences.

So Graham joined. He and Ginger knew each other of old, of course. At that time Graham was twenty-one, a wife-kid-mortgage, dynamic-young-salesman-verging-on-the-young-aspiring-executive man. He'd been around on the fringes for some time, and had been working with Don Rendell's Quintet for about a year. Ginger, Graham and I had played together many times.

Graham settled into Blues Inc. like a second home. In the twinkling of an eye he'd arranged with Alexis that he, Jack and Ginger should do a short organ spot in mid-set – that went like a rocket from its appearance. His impressiveness on alto was only added to by the power of his displays on organ and vocals.

Thus was formed Blues Incorporated Mark II: Alexis Korner: guitar and vocals; Graham Bond: alto, organ, vocals; Dick Heckstall-Smith: tenor sax; Johnny Parker: piano; Jack Bruce: string bass; Ginger Baker: drums.

Another indelible memory.

Blues Inc. did a lot of work round Christmas '62, but I was still doing a stint at the Flamingo whenever possible. I'd just done a Christmas Eve gig with Alexis at the Flamingo, followed by an all-nighter at the now-defunct Roaring Twenties in Carnaby Street with Georgie Fame. It was a long *long* all-nighter, and afterwards Georgie and I set off back to my place at 11 Miranda Road, Archway, on one of the first tubes of Christmas Day. As we emerged from the Northern Line into the daylight, we found that it had been snowing – three or four inches of it. The world looked utterly magical: new, white and beautiful. Georgie and I were the first humans on a brand-new Earth; ours were the very first footsteps. And we were bound for *bed*, dog-tired and happy. As we turned the corner into Miranda Road, Georgie stopped and carefully wrote 'Merry Christmas' with his finger in the virgin whiteness on the rear window of a parked Volks. I wonder whose it was.

4
The Beginning of the
Graham Bond Organization

By January or February of '63 it emerged that Graham, Jack and Ginger were going to strike out on their own; I remember Jack telling me one night in the tiny, cramped, memorable bandroom of the Flamingo while Georgie Fame and the Blue Flames rocked away outside, the glorious Red Reece propelling them ever onward from behind his drums. Was I going to go with them? he asked. No, I answered after some thought. I wanted to go on playing blues a while yet.

Alexis was apparently unperturbed; it was then that I began to appreciate the resilience of the man. His cool never seemed to blow. I did have a sneaking suspicion that he thought this kind of thing was happening too often, though . . . Anyway, before you could say Phil Seamen he was designing Blues Inc. Mark III.

The choice of bass player was, I suspect, largely up to Phil. The first post-Jack bassman was the magnificently talented Chris Thompson, a black Londoner. I always experienced Chris as a bright light: his intelligence shone everywhere. I'm sure it gave him a good deal of pain, too; intelligence can do that. If psychic and environmental circumstances combine unpleasantly, intelligence can contribute a good deal to the kind of discomfort that is killed stone-dead by drugs. Like Phil, Chris was a junky; and like Phil, he's now dead.

Before Graham left, he and Alexis had shared the singing; afterwards, the bulk of the vocals were taken over by Ronnie Jones, who'd been sitting in with us regularly. Black, and ex-USAAF, he'd settled in England for the time being; he looked good and sounded better, so that took care of the front-man aspect. But there was another problem connected with Graham's departure: while he was around the band had got used to having a horn section. Who was going to replace Graham the saxman? Who did I reckon was good on tenor?

'Who's got the balls?' asked Alexis.

'Art Themen,' I said without hesitation. Art had succeeded me in the Cambridge University Jazz Band.

Art Themen is the only person I know who has two completely unconnected professions, and is distinguished in both.

Imagine this scene: a drunken, sleepy, half-drugged blues band packed into a Dormobile, grinding back from Newcastle or Manchester or Liverpool in the middle of the night; Alexis is driving. (Remember that the M1 stopped at the Blue Boar, Watford Gap, in those days, and there were no other motorways.) There beside me, on the bench behind Alexis's head, is angelic, sober Art, reading an impressive medical tome by flashlight. It sometimes seemed to me that he had exams like most people have visits to the launderette. Well, now he's the pride of British tenor playing *and* the pride of British orthopaedics. I swear there isn't anybody like Art. He once told me he got off on doing things. Right! I remember him performing a minor operation on Phil's purple, swollen finger by the roadside one grey and shrivelled dawn – with a penknife. And, of course, no anaesthetic. Because – think about it! – Phil was already full of the most effective anaesthetic the world has ever seen, and it was having no effect . . . Phil bawled his head off and called Art all the names under the sun while the deed was done! But he was full of gratitude afterwards.

Spring '63 came and went; summer arrived. We worked more and more as time went on, and the band was changing its character. I didn't analyse this much at the time; I got on with things from day to day, enjoying what I enjoyed, like sex and music, and paying little attention to anything else. I wasn't the world's most penetrating thinker.

What was happening was, and to an extent still is, hard to disentangle.

The background against which my own little drama of musical development was unfolding was one of embattled musical divisions covering the whole scene. (I leave pop out of it for the moment.) On the one hand there were the folk clubs and the blues clubs, in which Alexis and Cyril had been working for some years. This was one division – folk *vs.* blues – about which I knew very little. On the other hand, there were the trad-jazz clubs and the modern-jazz clubs; they had their rivalries too, as I knew well, having crossed from one to the other before turning professional. Folk *vs.* blues; trad jazz *vs.* modern jazz. All four had their adherents, and a great deal of fervent, if blinkered, passion was spent in defence and attack – more, I fancy, than there is now, for which let us all be thankful. There was even a kind of 'soft–hard' division discernible as well, at right angles so to speak: folk and trad jazz could be seen as being at the 'soft' end, with blues and modern jazz at the 'hard'.

What I'd done when I joined Alexis was to change sides at the hard end. From a solid modern-jazz background I had transplanted myself into a blues band, and I'd done it for a reason, even if that reason was only an instinct at the time. The reason was approximately this: my musical development demanded that I, a jazzer and a modernist, should become a sore thumb learning not to stick out of a blues band. Why? Because the way I work, the way I have always worked as a musician, is as a blind animal responding to circumstance in the only way open to it. The consequence of this is that if I want to do something new, I must somehow arrange those circumstances so that they are strong enough to draw out of me music which I otherwise would not play; I must arrange to play with a band that will *compel* me. The exciting thing about

Blues Inc. Mark I had been that, as a band, it would not allow the fact that I was a saxophone player to overawe it into playing in the sort of 'jazzified' way that the presence of a saxophone would surreptitiously encourage. (There simply were no blues sax players then; they were all either rock'n'rollers or jazzers. My defection from the jazz ranks when I joined Alexis led some of my erstwhile mates in the jazz world to hint darkly that they'd suspected all along that I was really a rock'n'roller. A Commie in the State Department!)

What was happening – partly as a result of my influence, no doubt – was that as the personnel changes in Blues Incorporated gradually rolled on and more refugees from the jazz world joined us, my musical surroundings were getting jazzier and jazzier. Where I'd been happy being a sore thumb learning something new – how to be a blues saxophonist – I was now slightly less happy as a horn player in a bluesy, souly, pounding, shouting, exciting, slightly Mingus-oriented jazz group with a singer, however exciting it was. Blues Incorporated's jazzward progress was for me personally a regression.

Of course I didn't actually work any of this out at the time. Being of the non-analytic school of alcohol enthusiasts, I just played – and had a good time doing so, as the tracks we recorded then show. I certainly wasn't playing badly. Alexis noticed something, though. One day a little bird told me that Alexis thought I was 'losing my fire'; so in August 1963, about three minutes before I got the sack, I resigned.

All sorts of shit were flying in my life at the time, mainly of a domestic nature and caused by myself. The upshot was that after five months of marital chaos I left for Barcelona almost immediately on a personal mission, having heard at the last minute that Graham, Jack and Ginger wanted me to join them instead of John McLaughlin. John had apparently been sacked (by Ginger!) for 'speeding up'.

'Great,' I said. 'Yup. I've just got to go and find my wife first.'

'OK,' they said, 'fair enough then. See you when you get back.'

There's a lot to be said about the Graham Bond Organization, but I'm blowed if the words will come easily. I could talk about the members, the organizations we were involved with, the music, and the bizarre, often hilarious and sometimes horrific situations through which that music indomitably progressed, breasting the waves time after time, like – to quote McKinley Morganfield – 'a ship out on the sea'. But to be truthful, in my own mind anything I can say pales by comparison with the results of an imaginary conversation between the survivors: me, Ginger, Jack, Jon Hiseman, Mike Falana, and our successive roadies Brian Potter, Irish Jim, the two Pete Baileys, Manfred . . . imaginary, because it will never happen!

To anyone who was involved in it the subject is a live minefield. But a conspiracy of silence gets nobody anywhere, and there are a lot of lessons to be learnt.

For me the Graham Bond Organization encapsulates the Road. Not the romanticized and individualistic 'freedom' image that those two words have been used to conjure up since the fifties and the American beatniks – a very different, harder, more realistic image of the Road. Because the Road is the jazz musician's factory bench: the workplace.

The music business is first and foremost a *business*. A number of people with appropriate tools and skills, gathered at a particular workplace to invest their capacity to work in a specific kind of co-operative activity, the end result of which is salable. If the enterprise is to survive, some of the resulting money must go to the maintenance of the tools; if there's any left over, it goes towards the maintenance of the labourers, and with them their skills – not forgetting the part that goes to the public purse. So you see, for me and for many others the Road is the workplace. Nothing very exotic about that.

I suppose that the non-normal part of the music business stems from three things. First is that it comes alive when the great mass of other businesses go to sleep. Second is the peculiarity of its product: its function – its use-value, so to speak – is to affect people's minds directly, unlike the products of most businesses. Third is the inordinate amounts of money that go, very publicly, to a very small proportion of the labourers. But economics is always the framework. You may be the most glitteringly unusual character on the face of the planet, but if you don't make a living you'll soon be dead.

Well, the GBO made a living. From September '63 to July '67 we lived in a vortex of work. I have a vivid recollection – though unfortunately my diaries suggest it's a myth – that somewhere along the line we once did forty-two gigs in one month.

It would be tempting to serve up a few tasty mind-rotting drama sandwiches about those days, expunging the day-to-day detail that alone distinguishes one gig from the next, one Dormobile journey from the next, one hotel, or even one year from the next. I'll try a different tack.

In September 1963 we started with high hopes and plenty of confidence. The work was there, and by New Year's Eve 1964 we'd done 341 gigs in 477 days. The middle of '64 was quite a grind – fifty gigs in the fifty-four days from Tuesday 12 May to Saturday 4 July – and three of the four days off were consecutive. Then there were the recordings.

Our cashflow was interesting. The Bromel Club in Bromley paid the GBO £18 for a gig; Jazzshows, an in-town regular, paid £15. The daily income sheet in mid-1964 reads, '£35; £60; £30; £28; £28.10/-; £35; £25; £32; £50; £40', etc etc. Out of that came petrol, van maintenance and repairs (we were using an old ambulance, in which we did a thousand miles a week), hotels, agency commission, spares for instruments – strings, reeds, drum heads. It didn't leave a lot to be divided up.

Looking at that, and even allowing for an inflation factor of five or six times since then, I still wonder how and why on earth the GBO kept going.

At the beginning we weren't well known. But the link with Alexis helped, and the others had already been going out as the Graham Bond Quartet for six months. We kept our fees low, low enough to be working – promoters knew that if they took a flier they wouldn't lose too much. Every band had to do this to start with – they couldn't start any other way.

But we always went down well. The majority of the audience would go home having had a good time, so – we hoped – they'd remember the name and come back. It was a process of accumulation. The next time round we weren't quite so unknown; and most people weren't disappointed the second time round either. Reputations got built that way.

As long as the GBO was together, it always gave a good show; it was never short of a gig. And, most important, the music it was playing was not derivative – the GBO was not just one of a dozen bands that were more or less interchangeable. That meant that as long as we didn't fuck up, we kept working. And despite everything, we never did fuck up.

Round about November there was a palace rebellion. Ginger roundly spat out his opinion that Graham was a financial incompetent who had no idea of the meaning of money, and announced in the same breath of blistering invective that he would handle it from now on. Graham was very hurt indeed. As a man who'd given up a successful (if short) sales career in order to be a musician, and as the founder and front man of the group, he must have been trebly mortified: number one, his greater experience in the world of business had been dismissed and flung rudely back in his face as worthless; number two, purely as a salesman he'd signally failed to sell his business acumen to the rest of us; number three, he was supposed to be the leader anyway. There was an acrimonious fight, and Ginger took over the money. He handled it well. Then, in early '64, he handed it on to me with many detailed instructions. The trouble with that was that I didn't really want to do it. I didn't say so though. I just handled it very badly.

By this time I had begun to feel that I was the junior member. How so? I wasn't to start with. I had joined happily, and very much as an equal, both musically and as a person. It wasn't the case that the others no longer liked my playing, nor that they didn't like me personally – but something, somewhere, was edging me into a role that was not quite welcome to me . . . I think it was to do with the way that different personalities with different intoxicant regimes fit together. Somehow, the GBO as a unit found its stablest configuration with me as the Quiet One.

Anyone who works as part of a group, musical or otherwise, knows the kind of relationships that happen at work: work can be a hothouse. It's a commonplace of trades and businesses that people who aren't friends in the normal sense of the word – simply that they probably would not have chosen each other as mates – get to know each other better, in some ways, than they know their families and real friends. These are *working* relationships, and they happen in music just as in any other work setting; on the road, I suspect, they happen in a particularly intense form.

For a start, when you're on the road you're living a kaleidoscopic existence where one hour you'll be scraping for money, and the next the world is at your feet, with you cast as some kind of daemonic superbeing receiving the plaudits of a roomful of people, so you've got to do a good show however the fuck you feel – and an hour later, back to scraping. Added to that, you can never call in and say you're not coming in to work today – it just can't be done. There are no days off. Cold? Headache? Feeling poorly? Just had a shattering row with your spouse? Just feel effing bolshie and want to stay in bed? No way: forget it. You're four people boxed up in a tin container with wheels and an engine, and you have no choice. A sort of travelling open prison, a hothouse on wheels. For years on end.

Personal relationships under such circumstances can get pretty strange. Closeness, when untrammelled by friendship, can become very, very intense, both in nice ways and in nasty ways. My way of dealing with difficult situations – I was trained early in coping with a father with a very strong personality – is based on an extreme form of cussedness. Some call it self-centredness, but I have a problem with that – it doesn't seem to square with my extreme boredom with the subject of myself and my welfare. This cussedness expresses itself as a burning distaste for ever having my emotional state even to the slightest degree under the control of another person. I particularly dislike being made to be angry just because some stupid jumped-up berk takes it into his head to draw me into a quarrel whose only result is the pointless expenditure of emotional energy. I guess I've changed a bit

now, but then I was quite passionate about it. I possessed a diamond-hard all-consuming determination not to be moved into anger that wasn't of my own choosing. As a result I was no fun to quarrel with. I didn't play the game.

From the outside it looked like withdrawal, not caring. It wasn't, though. It was stubbornness. Ginger was one person who saw what it really was. There were a few times when he stubbed his toe against me, mostly in matters musical, and using his quick wits he recognized that under the facade of not caring, I was King Stubborn. I'll always remember a furious altercation I once had with Ginger in his front room in Neasden, his wife Liz looking on. We'd disagreed about something, and finally Ginger looked me in the eye and told me what he thought I was. 'Stupid bloody prat!' he snarled.

'Bollocks,' I said, enraged. 'Whatever else I am I'm not stupid. My IQ is a hundred and fucking forty-six!'

'That's got fucking nothing to do with it!' said Ginger. 'I didn't say you weren't intelligent, you stupid berk. I said you were *stupid*!'

'What are you on about?' I said, sensing a mysterious defeat around the corner. 'Stupid *means* unintelligent.'

'Nah! Twat! Grow up, will yer?' he snarled. 'It means in a fucking stupor, dunnit? Eh? Git!' He was always good at snarling.

I retired with a long face and we both drank our tea; it was as deft a killer blow as I've ever seen in a seminar. That was when I began to appreciate the value of semantics.

My absolute and impregnable refusal to get upset was a mechanism of self-preservation. Other people could be driven to the edge of sanity by the extraordinary pressures of the tiny world we lived in; I was never anywhere near it. I had learned not to attach enough importance to antagonistic interactions with other people to be driven anywhere by them.

I must have been a real pain sometimes. I put a lot of energy into the construction and maintenance of a flat calm external image, a homeostatically-controlled emotional state. Pro or con, it served: I survived. Thank goodness. One of the things that was preserved intact was a deep love for the companions with whom I had gone through so much.

One memory I have is a distinctly physical one – physical in the sense that I can recall it even now as a sensation in my body. A creepy feeling all about the shoulders, tensing up like carrying a burden. Anxiety. Not about anything in particular, just about everything in general.

During those weird Graham Bond years, rare anxiety-free moments were islands of balmy bliss. There weren't many things that didn't take place beneath a sea of anxiety, but it's wonderful how much one enjoys one's pleasures when there aren't many of them. Days off in the company of one's loved ones were rare; eating a good meal with plenty of time to enjoy it even rarer.

But there was a more frequent and more reliable form of relief from anxiety. Music, for me, has always been much clearer and more distinct, much less confusing and confused, than just about any kind of social life. And to be on the stand – before an audience, so that there's no chance of distraction from the music – that is bliss: a pleasure and a relief in itself. And oddly enough, that pleasure isn't at all the pleasure, or lack of it, one gets from the *quality* of the music! Musicians like me get physical pleasure simply from the act of making music. I always had a sardonic motto that, privately, I kept hanging over the entrance of my life. It went: The Safest Place in the World is on the Stand.

Funny thing about anxiety. If it's unrelenting enough and you are tough enough, it steels you. In the end you either go down or learn to put up a resistance, and in time you become as hard as nails, you're *all* resistance. By the time the GBO fell to pieces I could stay solidly on my feet regardless of anything any joker cared to sling. The weaker brethren always betrayed themselves sooner or later by losing their cool, being patheti-cally aggressive, attacking unreasonably – blowing it. These people – by far the majority – were those for whom I knew I had to make allowances. Dearly as I might love them, much as I might value them, when the chips were down they were not my equals. Baptism of fire . . . I've changed a lot since then, though: I've learned how to blow my top. I do it without fail whenever I give up smoking.

Another feature of a musician's existence – and not a million miles from the last in my opinion – is the way your work is concentrated into three hours instead of six or eight, and that these three hours come at the end of the day, after rather than before what we call 'leisure time'. Having it this way round does something to your 'leisure time' which robs it of reality. It becomes ghostly. The gig always looms at the end of it, an inevitable assignation. Followed, hopefully, by a biriani.

Musicians get to know this feeling and learn to live with it. It's a bit like travelling to meet your lover, knowing that even lovers can be a drag sometimes. Sometimes it really gets you down, like a drug that works below the level of consciousness. Once it's in there there's bugger all you can do bar cancel the gig. Some people try to make the situation more 'normal' by getting up late and going clubbing or whatnot in the small hours, but on the road this strategy fails due to the routines of hotels. Most musicians learn to live with screwed-up leisure time.

A change came over the band when Jack left. Ginger was quite adamant: the group would be much better off without Jack's 'disturbing' influence. I don't think Graham was quite so sure. I think that, like me, he felt cowed by the ferocity and the sheer unflinching obsessiveness of Ginger – for it was Ginger who alone had sacked Jack, and it was over a *personal* matter, the nature of which I cannot remember. Graham said little about it, and both he and I settled for an oil-on-troubled-waters approach. At bottom we both knew it was a *fait accompli*, if only because if Jack was somehow to come back into the band the resulting chemistry would see the whole band off. I've heard it said that Ginger's sacking of Jack was Stigwood-inspired, and was an early part of the putting together of Cream. An attractive thought in some ways, but such a machiavellian scheme would surely have been too accident-prone to have been seriously considered.

We worked on. Performances in some ways were now even more astonishing. They had to be, because with no bass player and only one singer, Graham now had to triumph over almost impossible odds. There was a kind of heroism about it.

We also took on a fourth member: Mike Falana, a diminutive, well-dressed Nigerian from a rich Lagos family. He was a wonderful trumpet player, who had been with the rest of us in '62 in the Johnny Burch Octet. He also had a wonderful attitude to Britain in its seamier aspects. We were travelling down an unprepossessing industrial valley in the north one day, little patches of green visible between terrace houses and factories, a pall of smoke hanging over the lot, when Mike looked out of the truck window and said, 'Byerraphall!' (it was how he pronounced 'beautiful'), 'fully automated!' Great little bloke. We've lost touch now.

5
Snowed In

A day in the life. Not exactly a normal day, but it does give a certain flavour.

It was January or February '66, after Jack had been kicked out. The band was me, Graham, Ginger and Mike. Our road manager at that time was Manfred, a young, tallish Austrian guy with spectacles. Capable, lively, a good driver.

The gig was in Carlisle on a Sunday night; the next gig was in Southampton the following Tuesday night. A day, a night, and the next day to get there in. Nice.

After the gig we stayed in a hotel in Carlisle, planning a daylong journey. It's a pleasant prospect to wake up in a hotel knowing you've got a longish trip *without* a gig at the end of it – so unusual it's verging on a holiday.

We planned to drive in a leisurely way to London on the Monday, sleep there – thus avoiding paying for a hotel, and drive to Southampton on Tuesday afternoon.

On Monday morning, however, we woke up to find it had snowed a lot. Remember, this was in the days before the M6.

Before the end of breakfast, Graham's getting an advance to cover his fare: he's off to get the train. There's a certain amount of red-rimmed snarling from Ginger about that, but the money's Graham's – it's off his wages and not even Ginger can stop that. So that's the end of Graham. Goodbye, Graham, see you in Southampton Tuesday. Mmmm. Could it be that Graham's a smart cookie? No no, forget it.

After breakfast the rest of us set off. There's a discussion about the route. Manfred maintains that since he's Austrian he knows all about driving on snow and suggests rather firmly that it would not be a good idea to go down the A6 with its dreaded Snake Pass, but to go round through Cumberland and rejoin at Kendal. I'm a bit agitated – wouldn't it be a good idea to get some chains? We vaguely look for chains in a few garages, but we don't find any – they've all been bought already. Anyway, there's a kind of undercurrent around that chains are namby-pamby, cissy, not British, not the sort of thing a real man who knows his way around needs to bother with: all this caution is just holding us up. Let's get on with it, eh? We've got a long way to go, you know. Manfred's clearly eager to have a nice invigorating Austrian battle with the elements.

So we're leaving Carlisle, driving along side roads. Quite slowly, because the snow is for the most part unbroken, nobody's driven anywhere yet, even though it is eleven in the morning. Well, we're going down some very dodgy-looking hills in our big van – the biggest of the Bedford four-wheelers, loaded to the gills – and it's got to be slow, even with an Austrian mountain goat at the wheel.

It starts to snow again – grey, darker now. A real snowstorm. We travel on, very slowly. Then comes what you might call a little taster. Going down one hill we start sliding sideways. The others are stoned by then, so they're having a good laugh about it. Manfred isn't stoned – he doesn't smoke – but Manfred is having a good laugh anyway because he knows how to handle snow. It's true, he does; but I'm not too cheerful. I'm not stoned either, and other people may well have wives and kids in London, but that in no way alters the fact that *I've* got a wife and kid in London. On we go. Slowly.

By late afternoon we're so far from civilization it's ridiculous. We're way out in the middle of the snowy wastes, going incredibly slowly up a long, long hill in completely unbroken snow. The wind is getting up, and it's hard to tell whether it's a snowstorm or whether it's just snow hammering and howling down off the mountains around us. It's beginning to get dark, the hill's getting steeper, the mountains are *up there*, and it's perfectly clear that we're not going to get over this.

But nobody wants to make the decision. Manfred seems to feel there's nothing to do but drive on, so he drives on.

Until, of course, the van stops, wheels deep in ice ruts, single rear tyres spinning easily on melted snow compressed into ice.

'Vell, zet's it,' said Manfred, turning to the rest of us, his spectacles glinting with triumph at his easy and practised grasp of the situation.

He switches the engine off. Zet vos indeet it. A truck full of gear and people, stationary on a mountainside in the dark, with a mighty force-nine snowstorm raging and ranting all around, visibility zero.

There's a quick panic confab – not a very coherent one. There's Manfred, perfectly straight, a relaxed, personable, humorous *Osterreicher* who's got us into this despite his obvious ability. There's me, straight, but feeling a bit worn down by being in this ship of fools at all. There's Mike Falana, who thinks everything technological is wonderful, and it's all perfectly safe in the hands of the wonderful white men up front. And there's Ginger, who's on a fucking trip, thank you very much! He's decided to have a trip because it's such a lovely day, he's going home, and he hasn't got a gig tonight. So he'll have a nice heavy dose of LSD.

Jee-*zuz*, it's nearly dark now. The snow is roaring down off the mountains . . . Manfred and I think we saw a light about half a mile back through the snowstorm, so we all pile out, put on what clothes we can, and carry one bag each. Ginger is completely wired – his face is red, his hair is red, his eyes are red – he doesn't seem too worried about anything. He and Manfred go careering off into the snow, following the fast-disappearing van tracks. Falana is very small; almost instantly there's a twenty-yard gap between him and the others. I split myself between him and them because I don't want a frozen-stiff Nigerian trumpet player on my conscience. He's so light, Falana, he keeps getting blown over, blown into

the side of the road with his trumpet case. So we keep going, further and further and further back.

There is indeed a light, in a completely snow-covered hotel with just one light showing.

Knock on the door, keep knocking on the door. Manfred and I hurriedly elbow Ginger out of the way because it's perfectly obvious that if anyone opens the door to *that* apparition, they'll shut it again pretty damn fast.

Eventually a woman opens the door. It's just her and her mother; the hotel's closed for the winter. I explain; Manfred explains in broken English – we both have problems since our faces are completely frozen up. All the time we're aware of this scowling six-foot reddish-purple stick-insect Thing loping about in the background, all snarls and big red eyes. We managed to talk our way in eventually, but imagine what it must have looked like to her! This loping, prowling stick-insect in back, and a tiny, neat little black man – in a *suit*, for God's sake? – getting blown over all the time . . .

Salvation. She's very, very nice; she takes pity on us, cooks something for us, opens up a couple of bedrooms. She even apologizes for the beds not being aired! We go to sleep and get up in the morning to bacon, eggs, fried bread and tomatoes. It's a good thing *some* people exist!

The next day it's sunny and the wind's gone down. Lovely. After breakfast Manfred and I go up to the truck, and it's practically invisible. A lump in the snow. The prospects of getting over the pass are zero, but we've got to do *something* because there's this gig. In Southampton. Tonight! Back to the hotel. Can we use your phone? Yes of course. In there. Police? Can you help us? No. The van belonging to the only policeman is snowed in. Can't do anything to help us, sorry.

There was an earth-mover, a snowed-up earth-mover on the road a bit back. It gives us ideas. The copper puts us on to a snowplough firm. Great. They'll see what they can do. We wait, and wait, and wait, and now it's getting dark again. By the time the snowplough comes and drags the truck back down the hill, it *is* dark. Dodgy business, dragging a loaded Bedford four-wheeler backwards down a snow-drifted mountain pass in the dark.

By this time we've phoned up the gig and left a message for Graham and the promoter: sorry, we can't make it. We're snowed in three hundred miles away.

Finally we get the thing dragged on to a road that's drivable, and during the evening we drive down Snake Pass and on towards Manchester, past Manchester to Stafford, and across the A5 – no M6 link then, it was still being built.

So we're on the A5 and it's late, two o'clock Wednesday morning. Manfred, who's done a great job of driving, is saying he's a little tired and what would we like to do? Stop a bit, or what?

Well, nobody wants to stop. But I don't drive and neither does Mike. That leaves Ginger. He's not quite through with the trip, but he's much nearer Earth than he was. He hasn't got a licence, but he has been learning. He says he'll take over so Manfred can get some kip on the passenger seat next to him.

There's no gainsaying this – nobody can stop Ginger. Mike thinks it's all right. He thinks *everything's* all right.

The idea of having a bloke with no licence driving the truck, and especially one who's on the remains of a trip – it was madness. There was so obviously a catastrophe waiting to happen that I nearly said OK, I'll take my wages and you can drop me off, I'll catch a train. I could have said it, but I didn't – it would have meant carrying my saxes, and they were heavy. So I stuck with Ginger's decision. I bit the bullet, trusted to luck.

The A5 was a very bad road then. It twiddled, it had a lot of humps in it, and since the M6 link was about to open, it was still carrying a lot of traffic *and* hadn't really been kept up as well as it might have been. It was narrow, too, with very steep verges.

To cut a long story short, Ginger loses control at about 45mph. He loses control because there's a damn pothole which causes the truck to swerve to the left – he wrenches the wheel to correct it, which brings it careering over the central white line, directly towards a pair of fast-approaching headlights –

fast-approaching death. So he wrenches it even more violently back again, at which crucial moment another exquisitely-placed pothole catches the left front wheel. The truck does a sort of pirouette and ends up half on the verge and half on the road, lying on its right-hand side with its roof facing the way we'd been coming from.

The little voice of Mike Falana is the first to be heard, piping up from under a pile of gear, light gear, thank God. 'It's all right!' he says reassuringly, 'Everything's all right.'

The second voice is Ginger's: 'You were driving, Manfred! Right?'

Ginger then proceeds to exit at near-luminal velocity by standing on Manfred's head and other handy protrusions.

Manfred gets out, I get out, Mike gets out, and . . . It's unbelievable when I look back on it. We simply walk down the road through the potholes and the rain, to a garage we can see in the distance. Eventually a guy comes out with a big truck, puts a grappler on the chassis and rights the whole van, just like that! Full of gear. Organ, Leslie, drums, PA, everything, all in this huge Bedford ambulance. Ger-*boom! Boom!* Boom, boom, boom . . . Bounces on its springs, the gear shifting about like lead shot in a maracca. And it's still going, believe it or not!

And Manfred's awake enough to drive. Surprise, surprise.

So we just drive on.

6
To be a Ruined Man
is Itself a Vocation

The next great milestone was Ginger's departure. Given the
20-20 vision of good old hindsight, I'd say that this was indeed
part of the construction of Cream. Ginger simply announced
he was leaving, and showed up with his first car, a brand-new
Rover 2000. His driving lessons were suddenly explained. He
was a little *piano* about how he'd got it – not exactly defensive,
just quiet – but it was a clear indication of a change in fortune.
It seemed he'd got an advance on royalties for a B-side of one
of the Who's singles, organized by Stigwood as part of a deal
with Kit Lambert, the Who's manager. Next thing, he was
gone.

Graham was in no way cowed. It seemed that through some
pretty funky after-hours negotiations – including some with
the legendary pianist/composer Mike Taylor, now dead – he
had already found an extraordinary young drummer called Jon
Hiseman. As I remember it, Jon joined at very short notice and
with no rehearsal, having heard the band and been persuaded
to give up his day-job by Graham's high-pressure sales
technique during one long night of rabbit.

Jon's pulsing wall-of-sound effect was large and immediate;
from the first night it loosened the band's feel. But his effects
on the band didn't stop with the musical. How could they? I

don't think any other character imaginable could have presented a starker contrast with Ginger. They had just about no personality traits in common, except in the matter of determination. Jon certainly had his own way of doing things. If anyone started with the naïve impression that Jon's anti-intoxicant stand was merely a result of lack of experience and opportunity, they would have been disappointed. I remember Graham, slipping easily into his venerable-greybeard-of-infinite-age-and-experience persona, telling Jon that he, Jon, was a 'dead ringer' – by which he meant that the configuration of Jon's personality would lead him inexorably on to heroin sooner or later. Jon was intrigued, and remained as bright-eyed as ever. As a prediction, of course, it was pathetic. Inspired seers run that risk.

It took less than a week for Jon to grasp the essence of the GBO's financial and contractual affairs, and less than another before he presented Graham – in the nicest possible way, naturally – with a choice. Either Jon took over the money or Graham had to find a new drummer. Jon took over the money.

As far as I was concerned, Jon's arrival marked the end of the who-dares-wins outward-bound trial-by-ordeal fearless-in-the-face-of-oncoming-disaster stage of my life. From then on, things began to get easier. The reason was that this venerable twenty-one-year-old was incurably sane. I too had hoarded little bits of sanity, jealously hidden away and guarded against intruders, and that made two of us – almost a majority.

We struck up a somewhat babes-in-the-wood friendship almost immediately. One of the first things we did was get into the habit of eating comfortably whenever possible. Once we'd delivered Graham to the gig, or at least offloaded him on to some suitable sycophant, we would creep off for a quiet, normal, middle-class three-course meal somewhere. During those meals we would have quiet, normal, middle-class conversations during the course of which nothing obscene happened, and no one raised his voice or manifested Strength of Personality, etc etc. Doesn't sound much of a thrill, does it? But scarcity value works wonders. (My stomach was rather pleased as well. After years of drunken/stoned Chinese/Indian meals alternating with fry-ups, flavoured as like as not with

daft yob-type rows, I was in clover. The effect of stone-cold fish and chips wolfed down fifteen minutes before the gig is something that has to be experienced to be believed: it sits malevolently all night long at the mathematical centre of the torso, gradually undergoing a sea-change as it reacts with the surrounding beer-whisky solution. The effect is roughly that of a reinforced concrete dirigible being slowly blown up to full size inside you.)

Anyway, to get back to the babes-in-the-wood conversations. One of the subjects we explored – somewhat whimsically it's true, seeing what our circumstances were – was the possibility of a band that had no passengers and no nutters. Was it really necessary, we wondered, that bands which produced great music should contain lunatics, lovable or otherwise? It was a joke, all right; we laughed uproariously. But it was a joke with an edge: a challenge. A *puzzle*. And it was the Graham Bond Organization which gave us that puzzle. The core of the puzzle was that the band – as a *band*, rather than a collection of individuals – was a volcano, ceaselessly spewing forth power and creativity, and at the same time it was somehow condemned never to see the success its potentialities deserved. A flawed volcano.

The switch towards sanity was inside my head, though. It certainly wasn't the case that my surroundings got any less crazed! No fear. In fact it was during the Hiseman year that some of the most far-fetched things took place, including Graham's legendary boat-trip up the Shannon with the two Pete Baileys, our father-and-son roadie team. The object was Coming Off, for Graham had intimated in no uncertain fashion to Jon, the Chancellor of the Exchequer (whom Mike Falana had christened 'The Oldest Young Man in the World'), that he had to finish with heroin for the benefit of the band, and that therefore it must be the band that paid: *he* hadn't got any money. Jon saw the iron logic of this, so the GBO ended up financing an Irish river holiday during which our leader would improve his health among friends – with, as it turned out, the aid of a restful tablet or seventeen of LSD.

It nearly broke Pete Bailey Senior. It did break the boat, apparently. And it seemed to me to render Graham as near clinically insane as it's possible to be without being committed.

When he got back from his Irish Hades, Graham summoned us all to Pete Bailey's home and delivered a two-hour lecture on the hideous profundity of his sufferings. I personally found it all completely credible, and at the same time oddly unaffecting. Throughout it, he seemed to be on the edge of physical violence; without ever actually saying it, he managed to convey the impression that he felt that his agony was not his fault but ours. And on top of that, there was something more worrying. For the first time he was without that expansive warmth that had been a part of him up till then; he had not a vestige of that larger-than-life, slightly ironic, self-deprecating sense of humour which had been such a powerful component of the man. In a word, he was unlovable; and that was quite new. Taut as a violin string, he chattered and barked and groaned the long and tortuous tale, calling Pete sternly to order from time to time whenever Pete showed signs of not supporting his version of events. As he talked I speculated as to whether he would still be able to play. It turned out in time that he could, of course, but the mere fact that I began to think like that was unprecedented. Looking back, I guess that was the moment when the actual physical end of the Graham Bond Organization first appeared in the distance. Some life seemed to have been taken out of Graham. His horizons had been cut.

Jon was horrified. He'd known roughly what to expect, of course, but I think that witnessing the devastation of this person shook him. However, his love and respect for Graham's music couldn't help but colour his attitude; typically, he spoke very little of his feelings at the time. But I think he was realizing that there was a price to be paid – and that price was too high.

We got Graham back on the road on some kind of even keel. There were tough moments, though. I remember arriving at a regular Norwich venue to find Graham spark out on an elderly sofa in the dressing room; we couldn't wake him no matter what, and the promoter said he didn't know how long Graham had been like that, but it was some time.

The gig was fine, of course . . . I remember one occasion when it wasn't, however. For some reason the promoter (not the same promoter) gave Graham a bottle of whisky before the gig; his perfectly well-intentioned gift happened to coincide with an acrimonious quarrel with Jon about the dreadful unfairness of a musician of Graham's stature getting so little money. The circumstances combined to give us a Graham who, having downed the bottle in twenty minutes, went on stage to become gradually robbed of his faculties – in particular his short-term memory – as the performance progressed. Towards the end he was (a) slowing everything down to a shambolic walking pace, (b) switching from number to number almost in mid-phrase, and (c) apparently unaware that anything was wrong. After the gig we drove a mumbling hulk back to the address he'd given us as his latest resting place – Oxford Road, off Ladbroke Grove – and deposited him fully clothed but unconscious on a bed we found that looked capable of supporting him. The next day we arrived at 3 p.m. to pick him up for the next gig, and there he was in the same clothes and the same position that we'd left him in thirteen hours before. We thought he might be dead.

I remember Jon, the wide-eyed, pleasant, intelligent, inno-cent but clear-headed twenty-one-year-old, being tormented by Pete Bailey Junior (he'd refused to pack Jon's drums after a gig). Suddenly, when I least expected it, Jon rounded on Pete and physically hung him up on a bandroom coathook by his collar and threatened him with an extra-special beating up if he heard so much as another whisper out of him. I was alarmed. From Ginger, yes. A normal mode of negotiation. But from civilized young Hiseman? I thought he must have taken leave of his senses. I tried to intercede, getting short shrift from a fire-and-brimstone-breathing Jon. Later he explained. The way he saw it, his one chance of getting the junior Bailey off his back was to appear to be more violent than young Pete, so he'd waited for the right moment and then 'lost his rag'. It worked a treat; Pete Junior and I both thought he really had lost it. If Pete had known it was planned it wouldn't have worked, though; Jon would genuinely have had to injure the lad to appear credible. As it was he got it by simulated loss of control and nobody got injured. A certain political acumen there.

Not long after the Shannon episode the band got involved with a guy from Polydor Records who had, perhaps a little rashly, let it be known that he might – just *might* – be interested in Graham. Jon and I did some groundwork first, then he wanted to meet the Man Himself. So we wheeled Graham in. Graham did a blinder on the guy. He was taken aback by the sheer g-force of it all, but it being 1966, things were fairly wide-open for undiscovered eccentric geniuses. Maybe he thought this impossible geezer standing before him *was* the next multi-million seller; maybe not. Anyhow, a deal was fondly patted into shape: £500 to make a record. Not a penny over the odds, but – in those days at least – it was enough to see an album in the can without the musicians' labour charges. Fine . . . So, thanks to Jon's hustling no-time-to-waste approach we went into Keith Grant's Olympic Studios at Barnes at the earliest possible opportunity, straight after a London gig, and did six hours' worth of music straight off, midnight through to six with scarcely an overdub. We treated the whole thing as if it was another gig, and there were the tapes, ready, just waiting to be paid for and picked up. All we needed was the money from Polydor.

But . . . very shortly, stone me if Graham didn't turn up for some gig or other, arrayed in the most extraordinary assortment of spiritually-significant finery – the kind of stuff the dribbles we'd been earning from gigs wouldn't have smelt a quarter of. Simply on the sartorial front he was a walking proclamation that something drastic had happened. Added to this, one look at the minces said loud and clear that he'd got hold of something extremely spiritually significant on the pharmaceutical front as well.

Oh yes. Disaster! Graham had gone into Polydor, taken the advance personally, and used it to rehook himself and acquire raiment adequate to the occasion. It was a *fait accompli*; there was absolutely nothing to be done. Presented with the extremely favourable £10-an-hour studio bill that Jon had managed to fix up through his contact with Keith Grant, Polydor firmly refused to acknowledge the necessity for abracadabra gowns and silver-topped canes; whether they tumbled the junk is anybody's guess. That was – sadly – that, for *we* couldn't pay; the band hadn't got a bloody thing. Olympic kept the tapes until somebody – perhaps it was Graham's American manager of three or four years later, who knows? – arranged for their issue on Warner Brothers' WS3001 as part of the double album *Solid Bond*. They're the nine Hiseman-produced tracks out of the twelve on the collection.

Graham, I think, fought hard but only partially successfully to stay away from heroin that year. I don't *know*, of course. He didn't discuss it with non-junkies like me. But from the lost, glazed look and the mawkish complaining that were so often in evidence, plus the rashes of inefficient and very poorly-paced drinking, I'd say it was obvious. Let me – as very definitely a 100% outsider – try to explain what I think was happening.

Heroin is a universal painkiller – accent on the 'universal'. It kills *all* pain, including mental pain; roughly speaking, what you might call the pain of unpleasant emotions. But, saith Darwinism, pain is not always a negative thing. It's there for a purpose, namely protection. You remove it at your peril.

Smack cures unpleasant emotion? Well, not quite. It's not that junkies don't feel emotion: as Graham would proclaim subtly, if magisterially, in his Peter Sellers Bloodnok voice: 'Ah! I feel no pain!' What happens is more like this. Junkies feel their emotions as if they were not theirs; they themselves do not personally feel the pain of their emotions. It is as if they were somehow an empathetic audience following the fortunes of a character whose life-events are being represented in an authentic and highly moving play being enacted before them. They are moved by the emotions of this character, and moved deeply – but they are moved *aesthetically*. The whole thing is at one remove, and like a theatre audience, they know that however tragic or harrowing or horrifying the play they are witnessing, they themselves are not going to have to face the consequences that the stage character would have to face if he or she were real. They know that before the night is out, the curtain will come down and they will slide out of the theatre and back into real life.

But the character on the stage *is* them, the play is their life, the curtain is the next fix, and real life is being stoned. It really is real, too. It's the life a junky shares with other junkies.

This leads on to something else. For better or worse, a junky has his or her emotions on cue at the right times and in appropriate situations – *but does not really feel them.* It can go on for years, just as long as the junky can hold it together. There is, of course, a price. It's paid when the junky goes straight. What happens is that all the years' and years' worth of unfelt emotions do not go away; they pile up. They wait, out of sight and deepening like a reservoir – thousands of tons of displaced emotions, a festering sludge of old and rotting feelings building up behind the dam of stonedness with nowhere to go. And when the dam is taken away, what's behind it comes out in a destructive tidal wave, monstrous and forever inappropriate – for what is there for it to be appropriate to? The situations that called this mass of inchoate feeling into being in the first place are long gone, ancient history. So the old, dislocated, dead emotions pour, stampede, devastate – out of control and unstoppable, stinking. So it was with Graham after the Shannon. It was rough. There wasn't much a bystander could do except let the man know that you're still *his* friend if he wants to be *your* friend.

At some point after the Shannon, Graham smelt the existence of Occult Secrets. Occult Secrets are hermetic, sacred, ancient wisdoms which come down to us despiritualized moderns in disguised forms. If we accept them in a spirit of open-minded humility, they can (a) make us worthy of our awesome but now lost spiritual inheritance and (b) give us supernatural spiritual power. Gorblimey.

Well, they suited Graham a treat – his very own Blast from the Past. After the Shannon he had a very open mind indeed,

100% ventilated, I should say; Occult Secrets filled the gap very nicely. Good old LSD hit him at about the same time, so starting with an open mind, Graham proceeded to expand the poor thing till just about anything could get in there. Terminal atrophy of the critical faculty . . .

Incidentally, for those who might enjoy it, here is a small Graham Bond story from a good deal later. I was told it independently by two people, and it seems to fit – though it's rather contrary to my own view of things.

When Graham went to the States, he passed through many Graham Bond-style vicissitudes before winding up with a manager who, it seems (and quite correctly, of course), advised him that since he was an alien with no work permit, he should bank any gig money he made in an account that could not be traced to him. He, the manager, would make it as safe as houses for Graham: he would open an account for him in a false name, viz 'Billy Gamble'. Graham gratefully complied; he did a couple of gigs, a couple of recording dates, made a crust and banked it. Safe as houses! Not even the Internal Revenue Service could get at it, and at last Graham's getting his head above water, finding his feet in the land of freedom and music, the land where the musician is king . . .

Comes the time to collect, and there isn't a cent in the account. Of course there isn't – the manager has drawn it all out. Of *course* he has! He was 'Billy Gamble'. So what next? Harken. What's next is: Graham sits up all night with a voodoo crony, putting a spell on the manager with much hermetic chanting, pins in dolls and so on. Next day, it transpires that, the very same night, the manager's wife had got drunk, gone out in the car and killed somebody in a car crash. After that, the manager is sacked from his job and ends up working as a barman.

I have something to convey about the changes Graham went through after the Shannon which is, for me at least, difficult to put into words. This is because it is not an event, not something specific which can be used as Evidence. It's something I sensed so strongly at the time, even if inarticulately, that in the intervening years other things have reminded me of it, producing massive clangs in my memory, even keeping me awake at odd moments – a rare feat. I shall hope to hint at it, give an impression of it. For starters, I quote someone very different from myself on the subject of someone very different from Graham Bond: T.S. Eliot, writing about Samuel Taylor Coleridge, a passage from *The Use of Poetry and the Use of Criticism*:

> Coleridge wrote the *Biographia Literaria* much later in life, when poetry, except for . . . one brief and touching lament for lost youth, had deserted him, and when the disastrous effects of long dissipation and stupefaction of his powers in transcendental metaphysics were bringing him to a state of lethargy. The *Biographia* is our principal document; and in connexion with that there is one piece of his formal verse which in its passionate self-revelation rises almost to the height of great poetry. I mean 'Dejection: An Ode'.

> There was a time when, though my path was rough,
>   This joy within me dallied with distress,
> And all my misfortunes were but as the stuff
>   Whence Fancy made me dream of happiness:
> For hope grew round me, like the twining vine,
> And fruits and foliage, not my own, seemed mine.
> But now affliction bows me down to earth:
> Nor care I that they rob me of my mirth;
>   But oh! each visitation
> Suspends what nature gave me at my birth,
>   My shaping spirit of imagination.
> For not to think of what I needs must feel,
>   But to be still and patient, all I can;
> And haply by abstruse research to steal
>   From my own nature all the natural man –
> This was my sole resource, my only plan:
> Till that which suits a part infects the whole,
> And now is almost grown the habit of my soul.

This ode was written by April 4th, 1802: the *Biographia* was not published for fifteen years after that. The lines strike my ear as one of the saddest of confessions that I have ever read. When I spoke of Coleridge as drugging himself with metaphysics I was thinking seriously of these his own words: 'haply by abstruse research to steal from my own nature all the natural man'. Coleridge was one of those unhappy persons – Donne, I suspect, was such another – of whom one might say, that if they had not been poets, they might have made something of their lives, might even have had a career; or conversely, that if they had not been interested in so many things, crossed by such diverse passions, they might have been great poets. It was better for Coleridge, as poet, to read books of travel and exploration than to read books of metaphysics and political economy. He did genuinely want to read books of metaphysics and political economy, for he had a certain talent for such subjects. But for a few years he had been visited by the Muse (I know of no poet to whom this hackneyed metaphor is better applicable) and thenceforth was a haunted man; for anyone who has ever been visited by the Muse is thenceforth haunted. He had no vocation for the religious life, for there again somebody like a Muse, or a much higher being, is to be invoked; he was condemned to know that the little poetry he had written was worth more than all he could do with the rest of his life. The author of *Biographia Literaria* was already a ruined man. Sometimes, however, to be a 'ruined man' is itself a vocation.

There are a lot of echoes in that.

Graham was a chameleon, many persons locked into one – not a lot different from the rest of us, just more so, perhaps. Over the decades there were many people who loved him – some for years, some for an hour. Each one knew a different Graham, and each was certain that the Graham they knew was the real one. So who was the Graham who was the sum of all these different Grahams? Well, if you ask that question you might get an answer, but I think that whatever the answer turns out to be, it'll be the wrong one – the mark of having asked the wrong question in the first place. Don Henley, ex-leader of the Eagles, was quoted in the *Daily Mirror* of 9 February 1985 as follows: 'We'd been touring constantly. I started taking cocaine, marijuana and opium and drinking vast quantities of alcohol just to get through. It affected some of the guys in the group really badly. Joe Walsh in particular became a really interesting bunch of fellas.' A felicitous typesetter's error?

I tell what I can of the Graham I think *I* knew.

'That which suits a part infects the whole, and now is almost grown the habit of my soul.' You can get into habits; you can even get into the habit of breaking habits just for the sake of it. Graham started his adult life early and was possessed of very many interests ('diverse passions'), and much bouncy, pushy, self-reliant, go-getting optimism. Inclined towards humour and happiness and with a more than normal 'weakness' for sincerity and human affection, confident of ultimate success at whatever he put his hand to and driven constantly to disprove in practice an internal principle of profound self-doubt, he somehow still succeeded in leading himself tortuously into a *habit* of failure. The smack and the occult ('drugging himself with metaphysics') were both, I think, aspects of this.

Many people come to hate their habits – Graham hated his as virulently as it's possible to hate an aspect of your life and yet stop short of rebuilding the edifice without it. After the dreamland slopes of junk there came, with the cold turkey and the Shannon, a grim, soggy, bitter discovery of irretrievable waste. The discovery didn't suit him at, all. It was as if the charmed one, the darling of the Earth, the ever-lucky gambler who always wins against impossible odds ('fruits and foliage not my own, seemed mine'), had risked his all – and lost it. The fakir had slept on spikes and cut himself; walked on red-hot coals and burned his heels. The occult was magically there at the right moment to help him retrieve what he had both lost and never really had – his birthright as Graham Bond the Winner.

But Graham had something else to his name, the heart of the problem: his talent. Very, very dodgy ground this: where personality and talent intermingle, full of monsters and fancy lights, a twilit marsh where the intrepid explorer can easily lose his way. Tough! I'll give it a go. The fact is – hold my nose and jump – I don't think Graham's relationship with his talent was a happy one. I think he had an enormous musical gift with which he could never come to terms, and I think that his fundamental difficulty with it was that he could neither comprehend it nor see from whence it came. Whatever qualities the incomprehensible may have, trustworthiness is not likely to be one of them. In short, this meant that he could neither trust it nor accept it. It simply possessed him. This state of affairs was as universal for Graham as the air he breathed, and as little questioned.

He dealt with his fear in two ways. One was straightforward denial, but of a rather subtle kind. There was part of him which believed all along that he was a fake and was deeply comforted by this belief since it meant that any success he might achieve was the result not of talent, but of his own personal efforts, efforts both of will and of salesmanship. In this way, the fear he felt was assuaged by assuming its cause out of existence, so that his abilities as a musician were on a par (as he gleefully and frequently claimed) with his having been one of the twenty-three best refrigerator salesmen in the United Kingdom at the age of eighteen. Thus part of 'my' Graham Bond was condemned never to know that the music he played was worth more than all he could do with the rest of his life.

But another part of him – deeper, more powerful, and therefore more urgently suppressed – was unable to sustain this comforting charade, since it knew, like Eliot's Coleridge, exactly how good he was. And that knowledge was dangerous: more than dangerous, it was literally insupportable. So insupportable was it that the part of him that was guilty of knowing it was banished, constantly under threat, constantly effaced, browbeaten, belittled. In a way, he felt both threatened and puzzled by being in *fact* better than he was in *theory*, as if he didn't consider himself worthy of being as good as he really was. It may be that the real core of the dangerous nature of the knowledge was this: if he *was* that good, but not as a result of his own efforts, then what was it a result of? And to that question there was no answer. There was no *reason* why he should be so good. It was simply intolerable.

For his own peace of mind he had to have reasons, even if only makeshift ones. At one point he believed it was his Jewish ancestry and became Jewish for a while. In his occult stage he discovered with excitement that in 1937 a Basildon servant girl was supposed to have had a child by Aleister Crowley; Graham, who came from Basildon and was born in 1937, became the Great Beast's secret offspring. Then of course there were drugs, and behind them,the wide, blurred concept of the 'addictive personality' – Graham was good because of the fruition of his pharmaceutical Destiny. He could never allow himself to be just good; he was always only good *because*. Some handle, however shabby, was better than no handle at all.

I have a friend who has a friend who was good – a genius, so they say – at making films. After fame hit him, people were always telling him how good he was, and gradually he (who knew the virtues and faults of his work better than anyone, of course) began to develop a persecution complex. People, he came to feel, were conspiring to lie to him about how good he was. He had a nervous breakdown, and when he had recovered he entered a totally different profession where he ardently pursued being an 'ordinary person' among 'ordinary people'. That guy may well have saved his sanity from irretrievable shipwreck, but he was different from Graham.

The difference is that Graham loved being told how good he was, because he took it as a personal compliment. He expanded and blossomed like a parched flower in the rain, for Graham – like the rest of us, only maybe more so – did not really exist for himself when he was out of his own sight, and other people were the mirror in which he confirmed for himself his own being. The trouble was that he confused being good with being thought to be good. Believing as he did (when the darker, more ruthlessly truthful side of him was comfortably suppressed) that being good was the result of his own efforts, he adopted the lifestyle that was supposed to be the right one for Pop Stars and Jazz Greats, and forthwith began to sacrifice both himself and others to it.

He was strangely innocent about this. God help him, he thought that to be *really* good, *really* successful, you had to actually *be* what people think Pop Stars are, twenty-four hours a day. The truth is that if you're aiming for a mass market, then your image is indeed a crucial part of the packaging. But that's all it is – an image. Real dyed-in-the-wool survivors in the big end of the music business recognize from the cradle upwards what's going on, and to some extent they learn to ham it up in public as a kind of protection for their private lives. Some say this is disgracefully Janus-faced; I disagree. I think it's no more hypocritical than putting on your clothes before going to work.

Good luck to all survivors, I say. But Graham was not a survivor; he was just *good*, more so than he knew. Open-minded, he swallowed the whole bloody issue lock stock and barrel. He didn't act the part, he lived it – and it killed him.

7
The End of the
Graham Bond Organization

The thing ground slowly downhill. Normal, routine difficulties piled up instead of getting solved, and the backlog of problems itself became more and more a convincing excuse for failure. Graham was getting harder to handle.

When a grown person no longer looks after him- or herself – leaving aside cases of clinical illness – it becomes less and less productive to do things for them; to make yourself responsible is to end up not only terrorizing your charge, but getting the blame for their failures as well. Sooner or later you have to get out from under. So it was with Jon and me in our joint efforts to keep the Graham Bond Organization afloat. Jon was the first to go, but the real end of the GBO came when I left, the last of Graham's original three companions to leave him. Shortly afterwards, Graham started calling his bands by other names. It was early summer, 1967.

A three- or four-day gap in our schedule was followed by three gigs in the north, the last of which was, I think, in Middlesbrough. Jon had departed a couple of weeks before, and Graham's personality was steamrollering about completely out of control, newly disencumbered of the Hiseman purse-strings. It was utter chaos. No one who hasn't experienced it could possibly imagine the full, imposing glory of

Graham's indiscriminate incompetence: he could rush head-long into disaster quicker than anyone I've ever known if there weren't enough dedicated people around to keep him at least slightly crushed. The young lad who replaced Jon on drums had no rehearsal and no chance, and neither did the eager young bass players, guitarists and so on who suddenly started appearing. At each gig, the band had different faces in it, and at each gig the repertoire was a new and more indecipherable species of soul bedlam, with Graham soaring like a demented Lord of Creation over the heads of the astonished multitude . . . and it's the band I'm talking about, not the audience! And with every gig it became more and more difficult to get paid.

I'd told Graham – and more to the point, I'd told Pete Bailey Senior – that I was leaving; to Pete alone I added that I'd worked out that I was owed £24, and that I was boracic and had to have it before I went. This was the real crux of the matter, for we all knew that with the new, post-Hiseman Bond on the loose, any talk of cash would bring a ten-minute paranoid diatribe about the diabolical liberty of even mentioning money to a Great Artist and Guardian of the Spirit of Humanity who'd been as shamefully ripped off as he, Graham, had – and by those who'd called themselves his friends, too (baleful glare) . . . etc, etc. There was only one way to get paid by Graham in the normal course of events: be there when he picked up the gig money and out-harass him. In these conditions, I naturally discounted the possibility of a rational discussion about what the band owed me. That was why I went to Pete.

While we were playing the Middlesbrough gig, Pete went backstage and looked through Graham's array of assorted chain-store carrier bags and disintegrating holdalls. In among the magic books, talismans, cloaks, boots, etc, he found an exercise book. Towards the back there was a blank page, with at the top the words 'Dick 24' in Graham's handwriting. In the midst of the screaming, hurtling, disaster-ridden circus that was his life, Graham knew all along what he owed me. There was more to Graham than met the eye and it wasn't magical either! I got my measly £24, and that was that. The end of the GBO.

Though it was the end of an epoch, nobody mourned it. There was no wake, no serious gathering to say farewell, not even a token handshaking session. It was all very down-market, conducted in matter-of-fact, nitpicking undertones.

Why did nobody, myself included, appear to have the slightest notion of the musical significance of what was coming to an end? Because it was disintegrating in ignominy, in slovenly scrabbling for pennies and inattention to detail? Maybe – the interaction of personalities was all that anybody seemed to be aware of at the time. I certainly didn't think of it as tragic then, and even now I can conceive of the tragic dimension of it only by imagining that it was somebody else it was happening to. Perhaps that's in the nature of tragedy. Perhaps it often doesn't feel like what it actually is to those scuttling under its heel. To me it didn't even feel like farce; it felt boring, tedious and small-minded – something to get out of fast, with no regrets.

In 1972, when I made my album *A Story Ended*, I had Graham on it; he seemed fine, if a little chaotic, but that was nothing new. He worked like a demon on the sessions, and we went our separate ways again. Then, in December 1973, I had a phone call from a young guy called John Hunt, who said he was Graham's friend-cum-manager-cum-roadie, and Graham was staying with him at the moment. Graham was a bit down – would I like to come and see him? He'd like to talk to his old friends.

Though I was in my first term at the South Bank Poly and up to my eyes in Social Sciences, I went round just as soon as I could arrange it. We met one evening at John's flat in Tollington Park. Straight away I sensed a profound change in Graham: it wasn't exactly that he was depressed – more quiet, distressed, worried; slow-moving but not relaxed. He wasn't happy. And, most unusual, not Graham at all: he seemed to have little or no impulse to talk. Instead, he wanted to listen. Specifically, he wanted to know what I thought he should do. I didn't answer him straight away; we talked together, quietly, over cups of tea, with John listening. After a while I said that it seemed to me that somewhere along the way he'd misplaced his personal confidence; perhaps he'd failed to separate it from his confidence as a musician.

I told him that as it happened he was indeed tremendously talented, but that his value as a person, independently of all the music, would have been just the same no matter what. Had there been no music in his life, Graham Bond would still have been Graham Bond. Perhaps, as Graham Bond the musician, he had undervalued Graham Bond the person; tied Graham Bond the person too closely to the fortunes of Graham Bond the musician.

Grasping rather at straws, I suggested that maybe he should get right out of the music profession for a while, take another job, any job where that Graham-Bond-the-Tortured-Genius-Guru disguise he was carrying around with him would be of no use. I suggested that he should find people who didn't know him from Adam. You're a likable enough bloke, I said. There'll be plenty of people who will accept you without the glittering prizes your music offers, without the carrot. Who knows? You might even get to like *yourself* without that carrot! Try it, I said, just try it. Graham nodded seriously. He was no fool; he knew what I was saying. I got the feeling, though, that he didn't like hearing it. There seemed to be so much invested in being a 'ruined man' that without the armoured carapace, the little pink human being inside was liable to curl up with sunburn the moment the unexpected eyebeam pinpointed it. I felt I had been cruel.

I had to go. I had a 9.30 lecture, and an essay to finish typing up before I went to bed.

That was the last time I saw Graham. In April 1974 I heard that he had died, violently, under a tube train at Finsbury Park Station.

Why have I spent so much time on Graham? Because he was so strong, so irresistible, had so much to offer the world — yet he couldn't look after himself, and he made it impossible for others to look after him. Also he seems to me to represent a lot of other people, and there are important lessons to be learnt by anyone involved in the public arts.

It's not been easy writing about Graham. I loved him too, and from a distance the task of writing about him looked very much like picking over the bones of a corpse, of a Graham Bond who can't speak for himself any more. From close up, though, it's not like that.

8
Interregnum: John Mayall's Bluesbreakers

A curiously blank expanse of time followed the dissolution of the GBO. It was summer '67; strange, unaccustomed things were going on inside the DHS cranium: rest, peace, slow-moving carefree sloth.

It wasn't particularly idyllic. It was just nothing. I was so acclimatized to battering, shattering dramas, to overwhelming total commitment to the band, that I'd come to rely on it. It had become a habit. In its absence I didn't know what to do, and didn't seem to care much either. I should have been up and out, worrying where the next penny was coming from, but I wasn't. I'd become accustomed to surviving by the skin of my teeth; underneath I expected to do the same again. And, by God, I did . . .

There was no freelance work, of course. The decision I'd taken in 1962, when I joined Alexis, came home to roost. The phone had been silent for years; why should it start now? It never crossed anyone's mind that I might be able to freelance again; it would have taken the best part of a year to build up freelance contacts to the point where I could live off them. So what was I going to do? A rented flat in Islington; a wife who, thank God, worked; a three-year-old son; and a musical ability that no one was paying for – so what now? I floated. One fine day I went off to Old Street to answer an advert for a truck-driving job, armed only with a very recently-acquired ordinary driving licence. Believe it or not, it had simply never occurred to me that I might need a heavy-goods licence: I'd never heard of HGVs. The bloke was quite kind, but rather short. The depth of my ignorance of the way the world outside the GBO worked was quite remarkable! In a way, I think there are some parallels with a serving soldier hitting civvy street. With the GBO as war . . .

Then, just as hell was about to blurt all over me, the phone rang. It was John Mayall.

It was a cracker. John had heard I was free – how would I like to join his band? In no time I was in my green 1956 Morris Oxford, belting round to Westbourne Grove to fetch him and Keef Hartley (Keef was the Bluesbreakers' drummer). John, affable and direct, settled matters in record time, and inside another hour I was running them both back again – with a job. And – I'll never live this one down – on the way back I asked my new employer for a quid to help with the petrol! It sounds nuts now. I can only think that being cooped up in the GBO for so long must have deprived me of all instincts about how the outside world worked. Definitely my most embarrassing memory.

I started pretty well immediately. The band was extremely free and easy rehearsal-wise: there weren't any. I simply went along to the first gig, at the Fishmonger's Arms, Wood Green, and played it, relying on the others – Keef Hartley (drums), Paul Williams (bass) and Mick Taylor (guitar) to do their bit, which they did. It was a relaxed affair – I've fallen off a few logs in my time, but this was the easiest of the lot. The other tenor player – long-nosed, sardonic, Afghan-hound-headed Chris Mercer, now settled in the USA – hissed a few crisply-capsuled pieces of vital information ('F sharp! Do what I do!'); Mayall gave a cheerful nod in my direction when it was my turn to solo; and it was all over quite painlessly. Talk about trouble-free. The audience welcomed me too, recognizing me from the GBO.

Pretty soon I heard how I came to get the Mayall phone call. The story was, apparently, that John – who had never had a horn section before – booked his by word of mouth rather than go through the tedium of auditions. Before long it became clear that something was amiss: the bloke who was in charge of the baritone couldn't play it. What he did was mime and ogle the talent near the bandstand; he did *look* good, of course – everyone was insistent on this point – but after a time, being the only saxophone player in a two-man section had begun to get Chris down. Eventually he'd spoken to John about his little problem, and when I came free, John had performed the necessary surgery.

There were two things about John Mayall that I quickly came to marvel at. First, his altogether admirable reputation, among both musicians and public, for autocratic monsterhood; and second, what a nice easygoing bloke he was. Where he got his hard-taskmaster image I have no idea whatsoever: from beginning to end he was absolutely no trouble at all as far as I was concerned. His *modus operandi* seemed to be: get the right players and leave them to it. The only musical instruction I ever got from him was that 'Right then, on you go!' look. In fact, the whole band was totally hassle-free to a man, and the contrast with my previous four years could not have been starker. Occasionally there was the odd complaint – naturally; there always is. Whenever I heard somebody described as being moody or difficult, I could only think to myself: ignorance was never more blissful, and long may it stay that way. And to cap it all, John paid noticeably better than the GBO; I was on thirty-fives straight away, going up to forties after a month or two. We were working hard – five, six, even sometimes seven gigs a week. And the bluesbreakers got me out of the UK for the first time since 1959; there was a Danish tour before Christmas.

Everything was going fine. I was playing and getting paid for it, *and* I was enjoying it. *And* . . .

But.

There was something missing.

What was missing was everything I'd had to cope with for the previous four years. *Everything*, from the white-hot screaming intensity of the GBO music, right on down to the white-hot screaming hassles of the team of which I'd been a part. Truly, there are indeed work relationships that are not friendships. I insist that they are not the same thing, since I know that friendships can be ended by work relationships. But friendship or no, work relationships can bring people so close together, at such white heat, that they become welded.

Believe it or not, I was actually missing the Graham Bond Organization. Not that I would ever have gone back had the opportunity arisen! Oh no . . . I was an ex-soldier missing the trenches – so used to the frenzied, punishing, lunatic microcosm that its eternal conflicts seemed no struggle. I suppose that when two kinds of life, two worlds, as unlike as those of the two bands are juxtaposed, then one of them has to seem unreal. In a way, then, the Mayall band seemed unreal to me – for a time, at least. My first, instinctive response to it – even to John himself – was that things could not possibly be as simple and straightforward as they seemed; such a convincing front must (I thought, or rather felt) conceal some real humdingers!

But no. No humdingers. The feeling receded gradually; as time passed the unreality lost its grip. By the time the next crisis was upon me – in summer 1968 – the world of the GBO had become a mad, sad, fascinating incomprehensibility that I had somehow been a part of in another life; a distant memory from another planet. It had become something which, whatever it had once been, now no longer lived with me. My whole conception of what was 'normal' had been altered.

In January 1968, John Mayall's Bluesbreakers did their first American tour. It was my first experience of the States – and quite an experience it was.

We arrived the day before we were due to open at the Cafe au GoGo in Bleecker Street, New York. We were to play there for two weeks – one club for two *weeks*! – quite enough of a culture shock in itself.

We fell straight into the Waverley Hotel in Washington

Square. The hotel was full of big old high-ceilinged seen-better-days rooms, with hardly any furniture, and a staff of roughneck militaristic cockroaches, violent, surly, self-important bastards who'd shoulder you out of the way as soon as look at you. (I exaggerate. There were cockroaches. They were American.) Downstairs, a curmudgeonly series of porters utterly failed to find the legendary quaintness of the English accent and old-world European courtesy in the slightest bit diverting. Restaurant? Breakfast? Service? Forget it, buddy.

I shared with Afghan Chris Mercer. It was like camping – best not to unpack, not even for a fortnight. We annoyed each other just slightly while getting on all right in general; just enough to enable us, married men both, to extract as much comradely privacy from the situation as there was to be had.

The day after we arrived we all trooped down to the GoGo and set up. We blew a couple of choruses for the benefit of the soundman, and that was it. We were ready to play in New York City.

Come early evening the waitresses trickled in. We ate, we played. In the interval I was rather preoccupied. We played again. By the end of the night I was in love, and I mean in love. I was head over heels, I was aflame! Quivering, I asked if I could walk her home. She told me she was 'legally married'. 'So am I,' I said, quivering. Her name was C— and she was French Canadian. She was the most beautiful, interesting, sexy woman I had ever clapped eyes on.

The next day we played again. I was still quivering. I asked her if we could meet the next afternon. Quivering, I met her as planned, and we walked, talked, went to bookshops, had a coffee. I walked her home. In Astor Place, quivering,

awestruck, overwhelmed, enraptured, enthralled, ecstatic, lyrical, hot-headed, impetuous, impatient, hysterical, delirious, overwrought, feverish, hectic, frenzied *(503 adj.)*, uncontrollable, emotional, passionate, intense, gushing, effusive, sentimental, romantic, mawkish, treacly, sloppy, thrilling, tingling, throbbing, blushing, flushing,

I asked if I could kiss her.

'Absolutely not,' she said with a broad smile. I quivered some more.

John, the indefatigable, made friends with Frank Zappa after the Mothers had played the GoGo – I went visiting with him once in the Zappa basement in the West Village. The front-room floor was paved with priceless blues singles. The penalty for a false step was never mentioned, but sobriety was definitely a *sine qua non*.

We all made our friends in different ways and different places. I got pretty tight with the zappy Jewish owner of a record store around the corner from the GoGo. One day he said to me, 'Come on kid, feel like a jam uptown?'

'Yeah.'

So after the gig that night – two or three in the morning – we piled in a taxi and went up to 125th: Harlem. A corner bar, black, completely black. I felt at home and relieved. It was just like the Flamingo All-Niters, only more so. Black music, black faces everywhere – my scene, my music. I remembered my best mate Eddie.

My record-store-owner friend knew the proprietor, and introduced us. The English accent did its thing here all right. Hostile blank black faces relaxed and turned to smiles as soon as it became apparent that I wasn't American. Five minutes later I was playing – on the stand again! The safest place in the world. I was happy.

I had a great night. I staggered back to the brusque, churlish cockroach legion at dawn. The next night the same thing happened, except that this time almost the whole band came. I didn't enjoy it as much – too many white faces. It meant we got segregated.

We left New York for LA . . .

A day later my heart broke, and I phoned. She was in, but it was dangerous phoning. So I wrote – letter after letter, addressed to a hastily-organized PO box. She wrote too – letter after letter, addressed to the extraordinary wedding cake of a hotel we were stationed in, the Chateau Marmont on Sunset.

Meanwhile we were playing at the Whisky a GoGo – more GoGo! – on Sunset. As first-timers, the band wasn't being paid much, and the owner very kindly made up for it by supplying free food and drink. Food, no problem, just order it. Drink, no problem, just tell the barman to put it on the slate. Fine!

One evening the owner appeared rather bashfully in the bandroom and spoke to John in a respectful murmur. Then he trickled out again, and John, amused, told all us chickabiddies what it was all about. From the size of the bar slates it was, it seemed, obvious that somebody was getting drinks for his non-band mates. The night before, one of the slates had come to *twenty-eight* friggin' dollars!! OK. Someone was taking advantage. Who?

Well, I knew whose it was. It was mine, and I hadn't bought a single drink for anyone else on it. The whole twenty-eight dollars was mine. I was proud, of course, both of my capacity and of the fact that not even the band had the faintest notion how large it was.

He threw back his tawny head and roared out that characteristic raucous Mancunian mirth of his, then asked me to moderate the intake. Better not strain the generosity of the owner. I reverted to a private bottle to supplement the slate.

On the plane I had taken it upon myself to deliver a philanthropic lecture about LA being Clap City to a captive, but not unreceptive, audience. Watch it, I said. Don't! And if you must, avoid the steamy young ones like the plague. Find yourself a nice respectable married woman whose husband is out of town, or your dick will drop off. Yeah yeah, they all said, you have a point. The band didn't have health insurance . . .

Come the event, everyone plunged happily into the nubile young groupies except me. In due course I plunged into exactly what I said I'd plunge into, a nice respectable married woman with two kids whose husband was out of town.

Why, you may well ask, did I do that if I was in love and phoning three thousand miles every day, writing long god-damn letters signed in blood? Well, people do that. My life was in turmoil and I was six thousand miles from home – for the first time, remember. Not only is being on tour in the USA a strange and disorientating experience, but LA is particularly nutty. A large part of me simply hadn't caught up with what was happening in my personal life. I suppose I wanted to see if I *could*; a kind of test, to see what would happen.

What happened was that a week or ten days later, when we'd moved on to San Francisco, my tool swelled up; and not one single other person in the band got the clap. I paid thirty good American dollars to lose my gonorrhoea . . .

I thought I'd better ring the respectable-two-kids-and-a-husband-who's-out-of-town connection and tell her the news.

'My gahd!' she said, audibly paling.

'It's true, I'm afraid,' I said, 'and it's got to be you because there hasn't been anybody else.'

'My *gahd*!' she wailed. 'That's *aaful*!' She sounded considerably more than just agitated.

A day later I noticed that the personable young executive from John's record company who'd been shepherding us to receptions and first nights suddenly looked very pale and drawn – quite unwell, as if he had a secret sorrow. I remembered he'd given my respectable connection a kind and neighbourly lift home one night.

My first and last dose. It put both me and my wallet in contact with the realities of gallivanting.

In San Francisco we were booked to do four gigs a week for two weeks at Bill Graham's Fillmore West. Coping manfully with the perpetual funds problem, John had saved some cash by bypassing hotels entirely. We were all billeted out, and I ended up in a house in Haight Ashbury. I couldn't have been more central to where it was All Happening; the house was a commune of flower people. It was brown rice and joints for breakfast, after which you Did Your Own Thing and Let It All Hang Out; I could scarcely take a step without banging my shin on a Spiritual Vibe. But sad to report, I didn't like it.

I don't want to be unfair. They were all extremely generous, warm, good-hearted people who certainly tried their hardest to make me feel at home. All the same, I had a problem: I didn't fit. The way I saw it, the household was far from being what it purported to be: free. Underneath the surface ideal of freedom, there was a complex structure of social codes. But, in deference to the ideal of freedom, these rules were unwritten; they were never articulated. Of course, and still in deference to the ideal,

one of the unwritten rules was that you must never ask what the unwritten rules were, since that would be to refer to their existence. To do *that* would have been quite horrific, since it would have been to call directly into question the reality of that delicate, fragile, surface pretence of freedom. It would have been openly, if innocently, to attack the *raison d'être* of the entire commune . . . Blimey, it was complicated. You just had to pick it up. Slowly and painfully, for I found the whole bloody issue somewhat oppressive – it reminded me, probably unfairly, of Graham's blasted 'spirituality' – I worked out that there were two fundamental rules of behaviour: one, no private property; two, no explicit rules. All the other rules were implicit and unwritten. Among the unwritten rules was one that said you must be nice all the time.

It's hard to be nice all the time! I didn't make it. Nor did I keep most of the other rules. I needed my solitude, especially then, what with being married with a kid *and* in love *and* having got the bloody clap from a third woman, to name but three rather heavy circumstances. Pretty soon I found myself in the invidious position of keeping myself to myself, asking for my own room, buying my own food etc, in the midst of a crowd of extremely nice, cheerful, outgoing, gregarious people who only wanted me to be happy like them. It was terrible behaviour by the standards of the house! I can still see the hurt in their eyes. I must have been 'weird'.

In among the multitude of scenes and events which seared themselves into my memory bank during those weeks – in the front rank – is the sight and sound of the mighty bluesman Albert King, our *support*, would you believe, at the Fillmore during our second week. The 'mighty' is to do with the sensation of having my whole corpus of entrails lifted and squeezed into a melting knot of heart-rending and sublime emotion, way beyond tears and laughter, way way beyond the reach of words. Albert King did it every time, and still does.

We had an hour's wait between flights at Kennedy on the way back. Very strange. She and I were only a few miles apart, yet – nothing.

By that time I guess I'd sorted myself out enough to be able to see what, sooner or later, I was going to have to do when I got home. Make sure Gary and Arthur (my son, then three and a half) were all right somehow, but not in the same place as me. It had been in my head for some time, but I hadn't recognized it for what it was, and certainly wouldn't have been pushed into it by anybody.

Twelve years later, when we'd been divorced for seven of them, I told Gary that I'd always felt guilty for walking out. She laughed, and said forcefully that if I hadn't, she surely would have done.

I suppose that our marriage had been weakening for years, though its growing weakness had been masked by the hard times with the GBO. Adversity acts like a bond sometimes (interesting how adversity and Bond go together). When things get better and the sun comes out, that bond dissolves away, and you suddenly find there's nothing holding you together.

My feelings about C— had brought it all into sharp focus, become the bottom line. Not that that on its own would have made such a difference, though I couldn't go on with my marriage *and* continue to have these feelings – it wasn't fair on Gary or me. Whatever it all meant, I needed to be alone for a bit.

When we arrived back I went to bed for a couple of weird jetlagged days. The life of a bandleader never stops, though, and by the time I got back in touch with John, Paul Williams had left, to be replaced by the young and talented Andy Fraser, soon to form the group Free.

In due course, we were back on the road, and soon there was another addition: Henry Lowther on trumpet and occasional violin. Life returned to normal. A couple of months passed, then quite suddenly Keef Hartley got the sack. The Hartley telephone sacking is enshrined for posterity in the first track of Keef's first album.

And guess what? Jon Hiseman, together with his old alumnus Tony Reeves on bass, joined the band. There was no song and dance or hullaballoo. As always with John Mayall, it just happened.

John asked me what I thought of Jon's drumming. I told him that where jazz and powerhouse rock were concerned it was all pluses, no minuses at all. In the field of blues I didn't know – he might have a problem knowing what to do, but his feel was great. I wanted Jon to join.

John wasn't at all dismayed. 'I'm sure it'll work out,' he said with that endearing coarse guffaw.

And it did. John Mayall's Bluesbreakers, now a seven-piece with a storming drummer and a three-man brass section, all of whom took solos, had changed a lot since the *Beano* days. That was the group that made *Bare Wires*.

Always an experimenter and DIY man, John made his own clothes a lot of the time, mostly out of skin and leather. Another preoccupation was recording things, and these two interests came together in the following way. One of John's less obtrusive vestments was a shaggy shoulder bag with a very shaggy shoulder strap. It never left him, and seemed to give him something to do with a nervous left hand – it was always slung across his chest, holding the strap.

Inside that bag was a portable tape recorder; inside the shaggy strap was its mike with an on-off switch. Whenever anything interesting was going on, John had it on tape. In the dark distant reaches of Porchester Road, all neatly edited, were the taped highlights of one man's life.

Somewhere on the Scandinavian tour the previous autumn John had had a strenuous encounter with an extrovert and powerfully-built blonde woman on a trip, who had had a good deal of stamina. This had happened on a hotel bed whose springs were extremely pressure-sensitive. Beneath it all, throughout, was John's shaggy shoulder bag, with the mike switch left on. It was all part of the action.

Well, in the *Bare Wires* studio, John produced a six- or seven-minute edited two-track version featuring choice rhythmic subtleties culled from the original state-of-nature magnetic, strung together to form a whole, with a beginning, a middle and an end. Instructing Jon Hiseman to play to what he heard, he sent the lad into the studio and fed this *rythme trouvé* into his cans without further explanation. Jon, the ultimate responder, did a series of masterly performances. John chose the one he liked best, and used it as the basic backing track for a song called 'Fire'. It's on *Bare Wires*, and I'm told the original two-track is present in the mix as well: now you hear it, now you don't. John is sometimes accused of copying the black greats of the blues. Well, 'Fire' *is* a blues number of course, but it's hardly what you'd call slavish imitation.

About a fortnight after Jon joined, we were in the band bus travelling between gigs. The usual scene – bodies slumped in various states of glazed vacancy, Mick Lawford the roadie (or was it Col Smith that day?) eating up the miles with his foot on the tranny floor and his eyes thirty yards ahead.

Suddenly the Hiseman tones suffused the air with humanity, addressing John affably from the back of the bus. He proceeded to explain to John that he, as a self-manager, was ripping himself off.

'Look at it,' he said. 'I haven't been with this band long, but I've been with it long enough to see that you're doing the same circuit Dick and I played with Graham a year ago, and I know what they charge on the door is the same, so I know what they're paying, and let me tell you, you're undercharging. We played these venues for a year, and we never once attracted half the number you attract. You play to overflowing houses every time you care to put your nose outside the door, John, but I'll lay odds you're in the same price bracket! I've seen queues halfway round the block, John, and you know what? Half those people never get in to see you at all. Yet you're working your bollocks off to pay the wages. How long have you been on the road now, John?'

'Four years,' said John, grinning.

'OK,' said Jon, 'and who decides what your fees are?'

'I don't know. I suppose I do, and the Gunnell Agency does,' said John, grinning some more, intrigued.

Jon snorted with a kind of gleeful venom. 'The Gunnells,' he said. 'The best thing you can do is get in there first thing tomorrow, John, and pull out every gig that isn't signed, starting yesterday. And then tell those shysters to get on the blower and tell every single one of those promoters that your fees have doubled overnight. That way they'll have to hire bigger venues or else charge double on the door. Hit 'em where it hurts, they can afford it, most of 'em. Oh they'll shout all right! The Gunnells'll squeal, the promoters'll squawk till their voices break – but I guarantee they'll be back, all of 'em to a man. I'll lay odds on that. You've been everybody's friend for too long, John.'

And with that the bright-eyed young whippersnapper returned to his previous silence, satisfied. Take it or leave it.

John said nothing; neither did anyone else. But very shortly afterwards a grinning John Mayall appeared in the truck and announced, 'I've done it!'

Done what? we all mumbled.

'Blown the office up. Pulled out all the gigs and doubled all the fees. You should've seen 'em!' he cackled. 'Now we'll see whether you're right or not,' he added, shooting a look at Jon.

Well, it worked. Jon Hiseman *was* right. For a while the work dropped off in sheer volume, but the wages stayed the same. Then the work climbed quickly back to where it had been before, and the wages went up.

9
The Rise of Colosseum

By the time Jon joined the Bluesbreakers, the GBO climate inside my head had become a distant memory, recallable only as an eerie curiosity. The interregnum had done its work, for here I was, already embarking on my next crisis; Jon and I scarcely talked at all about our mutual past. Once or twice, though, we did return to that no-passengers-no-nutters dream of ours. Jon was the one who most closely shared the same passionately rebellious feelings on the subject that I kept hidden, simmering until their moment came. With Jon as an ally, I began to think, it might actually stand a chance.

Around the end of July 1968, John Mayall decided once again that he was going to renovate the band – keep the content but alter the form; leave the music basically the same but change the personnel. He wanted to go right back to a quartet format, make it as quiet as possible, carry a very small PA.

So. Number one: out with the brass! A completely different set-up for the autumn American tour, and the end of me, Chris and Henry.

Just possibly not, though . . . Shortly after the bombshell, John got me and Mickey Taylor together and told us that the new quartet's featured soloist would be either a saxophone or a guitar. The idea of a sax was attractive, he said, but he wasn't sure whether the time was ripe yet; he didn't know whether he had the bottle for such a major innovation as a guitarless blues quartet. (He played guitar himself, of course, but we knew what he meant. Most of the time he played keyboards.)

'It's going to be one of you two,' he said with yet another Mancunian guffaw. 'I'll let you know which one in a week.'

One sunny evening before a South London gig he found me warming up alone in the dressing room. 'Hullo, Dick – it's bad news, I'm afraid.'

So I was definitely out. I'd just left Gary; I was living in a room in Fulham on my own; I had not the slightest idea what was going to happen next. I went to Hiseman on one of the last gigs and said: 'Hey Jon, I don't know what I'm going to do now, but sure as hell I'm going to have to do something PDQ or I'll be dead. If we're ever going to form this band of ours, it's got to be now.' To which he replied that John had asked him to stay on for the American tour, but that would be over in three months. 'Three months is too long,' I said. 'If I'm still alive, I'll be committed to something else. Think about it and let me know fast.'

He phoned me back a couple of days later. 'Dick,' he said, 'I've thought about it and I'm sorry, but the answer is no. I want to do the American tour. Hope you're still around when I get back.'

'OK, fair enough,' I said, 'see you then.'

So that was that. I scurried around trying to find a gig, and occupied myself with my private life. Just before I got the sack, C— had come to Britain for a two-week holiday which expanded to six. I had just eighty pounds; mostly we went for walks or stayed in the Fulham place, trying not to spend it. I have to say: it was idyllic.

A couple of weeks later the phone rang in the Fulham hallway. It was Jon. 'OK,' he said crisply, 'I've given in my notice. I've got a band; I've got rehearsal time booked. I've negotiated management and agency contracts. Are you in?' There was no hesitation! I was in, all right.

Rehearsals got under way in a festive and enthusiastic atmosphere, on schedule. From then on everything ran, if not always smoothly, then at least according to plan. Gerry Bron, the person Jon had in mind as manager, came to one of the early rehearsals at St Stephen's Church Hall, Elephant and Castle, accompanied by Colin Richardson. Colin had been Jon's contact in the first place. According to Colin, Gerry's face lit up when he first heard what we were playing: he'd been expecting another soggy if workmanlike post-Bluesbreakers offshoot.

In fact, of course, the band was incomplete. We had Jon on drums, Dave Greenslade on keyboards, Tony Reeves on bass, and myself. We had neither a singer nor a guitarist, and our first task was to arrange auditions with the aim of finding a singer/guitarist – a nice compact five-piece. An advert went into the *Melody Maker*, replies to the office please; and in very short order Gerry Bron's beautiful, efficient, soignée secretary Jan was on the receiving end of upwards of 250 hopeful applications from all over the country. What a heroine! How she did it remains a mystery to me, but she quickly reduced the number to fifty-four. So during three hectic days at the end of August, we started the serious business of Colosseum by shepherding fifty-four young blokes through two twelve-bar blues each.

What an experience. Never again! Everyone in the band aged ten years. Grey parchment skin hanging off emaciated cheeks; black hollows round staring, crazed eyes.

Dave Greenslade retired to bed after it was all over, a dead man for three days. As the keyboard man, it was Dave who had the gig of checking each guy's tuning . . . There was one of them – a Geordie with hair that covered the front of his head completely, let alone the back – who wandered up with a home-made guitar.

'Want an E?' asked Dave.

'Nah,' said the front of the guy's head, 'it's all right, it's great man, it's in tune, I made it myself.'

'Oh well, give us an E anyway,' said Dave with an inward sigh.

Boinggg! Miles out – 'spot off' as we gnarled old jazzers say.

'I always had trouble with this E,' said the bloke.

Then there was Flashing Fingers. He had a green velvet suit

and glamorous blond hair, and he looked *magnificent*. We saw him coming miles off, waiting in line down at the far end of the hall with the rest – you couldn't miss him.

'Wow,' we murmured among ourselves, 'we've got to get to him! Nobody who isn't great would have the bottle to dress like that! He's *got* to be *great!*'

He had a great steaming brute of an axe, too. When we finally worked our way through to him we never heard a note; it was all *brrrr-brrrr zing click*, up and down the scales, and so goddamn quiet that nothing came out. We got him to turn it up, and played a slow blues in the hope of hearing something. Still nothing; just *brrrr-brrrr zing click*. Weird. Nice bloke too, very affable and all that; great charisma. Wonder who he was . . .

The upshot was not one guitarist but two: James Litherland and Jim Roche. Their styles were a nice contrast, and James's vocals were strong and soulful. Gutsy, and with a particular hoarse yet youthful voice quality that I never heard from anyone else until Sting appeared.

Rehearsals proper lasted a month: August through to September, with the third week a short one to let Jon clear up loose ends on the business side. The office kept a paternal eye on us, appearing more than satisfied; there was quite a respectable amount of interest among promoters.

Meanwhile, one fine (jobless) day towards the end of that turbulent summer, I happened to be walking down Charing Cross Road with not a lot in view, when I found my way blocked by the wide and ferociously bearded benevolence of someone I'd known, on and off, for over a decade: John Jack, a rubicund, all-knowing ex-trombone player, now entrepreneur, aficionado and general man-about-jazz.

'Ah, dear boy! How are you?' John always did talk like that. He'd become an *eminence grise* the day he got the vote; it suited him a treat, as did his duffle coat. He was no older than me, actually.

I was pleased to see him; he brightened my day. 'Well now, young feller-me-lad! Just the chap I was looking for. Would you perhaps care to do a gig for me? I am fortunate enough to find myself to a certain extent in cahoots with the famed 100 Club.'

A gig! Wow, was I pleased to see him. 'Blimey! Yeah!' I shrieked. 'When? What's the bread like?'

He expanded visibly. 'Merely an interval spot, I fear. The fiscal dispensations may not possibly run to very much. But I note that you are, shall we say, *resting* as of this particular point in time; isn't that so? How say you?'

I didn't hesitate. 'How about a trio?' I'd been fancying the notion of Jack Bruce, Jon Hiseman and myself blasting hell out of some music somewhere, for quite a time – months, as it happened.

'Excellent! Expect a call, dear boy,' said John. We parted cheerfully.

The call came in due course. I rang Jon and Jack; both of them said yes to the date in question.

Came the day. All three of us showed up, did the gig. It was just a short set, filling in the support spot for a band about which I can remember nothing except that in the matter of styles it was a wild contrast to the kind of thing we were up to. Ours was a real rip-roaring no-prisoners set with only the barest of perfunctory nods towards anything like a tune, and all three of us were dripping with sweat and ecstasy when our half-hour was up. We fell, ululating, on one another's necks and swore we must do it again somehow.

Well, that trio never did do another gig of course; there was too much else happening. But not long after, I got a call from Jack saying he'd got money from Stigwood (his manager) to do anything he liked for his next album – and he wanted to do it with the trio! He was as good as his word. He and I got together at his flat to blow through some lines that he'd written, believe it or not, when he was eleven, and to cut a long story short, the album was cut in three days at IBC studios, Portland Place, in August.

While it was being recorded John McLaughlin appeared at Pete Brown's flat in Montague Square, where I was staying after C— left for New York. John had just returned from New York himself, as quiet, troubled and uncertain as ever (this was before he joined Miles). He and I had known each other since 1960 or '61, when he was a fresh-faced young innocent discovering cannabis resin and, no doubt, lots of other things, in Georgie Fame's Blue Flames, and I was doing the intervals in the Flamingo All-Niters. Over cups of tea in Pete's kitchen we talked over the years of separation before tottering off to bed.

When I got to the session in the morning, I told the others. The upshot: a phone call, and half an hour later, there he was! John Mac, plus guitar and an absolutely minute, fucked-up practice amp that made an absolutely minute, fucked-up noise which, recorded and played back loud, sounded out of this world.

And that was it, basically. John just joined in, without rehearsal. And the results? They are to be heard on the Jack Bruce album *Things We Like*. It is one of the very few recordings I've made that I like.

That's the real story behind the fact that John McLaughlin isn't on all the tracks of *Things We Like*. He didn't even know about it until we were halfway through recording.

At the beginning of October, Colosseum went on the road. We went down well from the off, it seemed. The office feedback was very positive. One thing we did was take a difficult but necessary decision and lose one of our two guitarists; Jim Roche left for two reasons: one, he wasn't settling down with the band solo-wise the way we'd expected from his performance in rehearsal; second, he didn't sing and James did. After a month we came off the road in order to plunge into a concentrated spasm of rehearsal, during which we ditched failures, polished up successes, and added new material; then, back on the road. In three heavy days at the start of November, we went into the studios and came out with the first Colosseum album: *Morituri Te Salutant*, or *Those About to Die Salute You*. It hardly needs explaining, does it? That was the form of words with which, in Rome's days of imperial glory, the Colosseum's slave gladiators were supposed to dedicate their unfortunate souls to the current Caesar as they were marched out into the arena for the entertainment of the free citizens. It was a subtle way of laying a small bet against ourselves: if we did die, then that's what we had said we'd do, wasn't it? And if we were a resounding success – then who cares anyway? They were heady days.

Christmas came and went in a vortex of work; I never noticed it. The first half of 1969 was prolonged and intense hard labour around the UK, and on 16, 17 and 18 June we went into the IBC studios to make the second album. Again a three-day LP, excluding mixing. Then came a real snip, which the office had achieved rather late in the day: the Montreux Festival on Saturday 21 and Sunday 22 June. We did one scheduled concert and one unscheduled one, ending up playing by the hotel poolside in sun so hot that I celebrated by shedding as many clothes as I could and plunging into the pool. After the gig, that is.

That little escapade was followed by a dash home to do Exeter on the 27th – Friday – and a double on the 28th, the Bath Festival in the afternoon plus the Van Dyck Club in Plymouth in the evening.

And *then*: America. We travelled on 8 August, and I saw C— for the first time in a year. It was a shoestring, real-hard-graft tour, for which the office had exceeded all its previous efforts. Considering the difficulties they had faced, with Jon involved up to his neck every step of the way as the bandleader, it was just short of a miracle that nothing went awry.

What a kaleidoscope. Three days in Boston were our introduction, the 11th to 13th; then four days at Bill Graham's Fillmore West – the selfsame Fillmore West where I'd played the year before with John Mayall, alongside Albert King. Then the 19th to the 24th at the Los Angeles Whisky a GoGo; more shades of the Bluesbreakers. Then slap bang back across, coast-to-coast, with the 26th to 28th at Ungano's on Manhattan's upper west side, followed by the 29th and 30th at the Grand Ballroom, Detroit. Then came a funny little one-off at an Anthony Perkins-style nissen hut in Massachusetts – a local dancehall about which I can't remember much, except that it seemed to me unglamorous and somewhat threatening. And then, finally, September the 2nd to 7th in Lower Manhattan again: six days at the Electric Circus in St Mark's Place, East Village. Almost opposite C—'s flat.

One of the most vivid memories of my life is of a funny little moment in that extraordinary place, the Electric Circus. I was playing alone, centre stage in a pool of light, with my eyes – as always – shut. I felt, rather than heard, the room sound of the saxophone alter subtly in a way I knew I was not responsible for, and I opened my eyes. There was a guy directly in front of me, crammed against the proscenium on which I stood, and he, believe it or not, was stealthily moving the microphone stand away from the bell of my horn. He thought I hadn't noticed, I guess. I stamped on his fingers. That was that – no further interference. I thought no more of it until after the gig, when various wellwishers suggested that perhaps I might be wise to exercise caution. Nothing happened, and I never saw nor heard of him again. I hope his hand recovered!

Then straight home, thank God. Four days off, and back to work, with C— arriving in the middle of rehearsals to stay for good. It was during the next two months that we dealt with our first personnel change: James Litherland left to put into action plans for a group of his own, which later became Mogul Thrash. His replacement was the young leader of Bakerloo, Dave ('Clem') Clempson, who was to stay with Colosseum until its death. Clem quickly fitted in, his innate musicality showing in everything he did, and after that Colosseum played and played and never seemed to stop.

Clem's first taste of Colosseum life was a European tour – a gig in Prague on Saturday 1 November. It was, I remember, wonderful musically, and very emotional: the band soared. And during it Clem's glittering new guitar case was stolen.

It was my second visit to the Evil Empire, as Ronnie Reagan has so eloquently christened it – the land beyond the Iron Curtain. My first had been a decade earlier, when – ultimately under the auspices of the US State Department – I'd played baritone sax for Jerome Robbins's Ballets USA, in the Palace of Culture in Warsaw.

A letter I wrote home from Prague remarks:

It's ten degrees colder in Praha than in London – cold strong wind, mist, iron-grey overcast skies when I got off the plane. One piece of gear lost – delay – found; taxi to Prague, taxi driver gives long lecture on dire effects of Russians in Czechoslovakia. Says if you're (a) stupid and (b) communist you're happy, and only one half of one per cent is. Ninety-nine per cent are unhappy and have nothing. Says one year ago everything was fine in Cz., and that everything changed completely in two days: now he hasn't got a passport. That's all he wants and he can't get it.

I must say I can no longer remember that incident. In fact I recall a few disjointed impressions very strongly indeed, and virtually nothing else. A sad bookshop in a Prague square with only one book on display in its window. Being abducted by sheer force of pleading to a tiny bare second-floor Saturday-afternoon jazz club, and playing there with my gentle, grateful, studious captors. An eager, bespectacled Hungarian kid, rather like Alfred E. Newman, who adored all things Western and stuck desperately close to Colosseum for as long as he could, promising he would see us again in the West; he was indeed heard of later in a North Italian refugee camp. I still have photos that have him in them.

One thing I do remember is an incident, small in itself but large in that it was a brush with real life-and-death politics, that actually happened in the gig itself. But before I get to it I'd like, with the reader's permission, to say something about the context in which it took place.

The picture we have in the West of what happened in Czechoslovakia in August 1968 is pretty much the one implied in that taxi driver's long lecture. Very briefly, it's one of brutal Russian tanks crushing the new and delicate flowers of Czech freedom. It's no part of my business to deny the truth of this image. Instead, I believe that we should, if we are wise, add to it another, and I would like to introduce that other image with a comment that comes from the Dick Heckstall-Smith who is writing a book in the eighties, and not from that distant namesake of his who travelled to Prague in the late sixties.

Throughout the writing of this book I've had in mind the fact that the life I'm writing about was lived in the context of a world full to the brim with historical events of which I was, at the time, determinedly unaware. Let me enlarge on that a little. The events I am talking about were enormous; they were gigantic, titanic shiftings in the economic and political, ideological and military currents of human life on this planet, and they seemed to have nothing whatever to do with me. My unawareness of them was more than ignorance; it was a positive thing. For me at that time, politics – in fact anything intellectual, but most of all politics – were the perfect no-no, the ultimate turn-off. This was a territory that was distasteful to my whole cast of mind and to my experience. It managed to be at one and the same time both grey and boring, and forbidding and incomprehensible. I didn't want to know. In the face of anything remotely political I was humble, resentful, inarticulate and glazed.

To me now, this fact of my early life – my life up to the age of forty – is immensely significant, charged with a significance that far exceeds the boundaries of any one single life. For I was not alone in how I felt, or rather didn't feel, about politics. I was one of many, many millions of individuals in relatively liberal, comfortably-off countries who felt pretty much as I did; individuals who were assumed, by themselves and others, to have entered upon their adult lives equipped with the advantages of a well-rounded if basic-minimum education, yet for whom the political life of the planet was an unattractive and threatening mystery, the details of which could be neatly despatched from sight and mind by means of useful rules of thumb about 'leaders', 'politicians', 'human nature', or even, heaven help us, racial and national characteristics, though this last was never one of my standbys. I was one of the millions upon teeming millions of more or less averagely intelligent, more or less averagely sophisticated, competent individuals for whom the politics of the world were a blindspot.

And why is this important? It is important because the ponderous dead weight of inertia generated by the over-arching 'apolitical' orthodoxy in the wealthier nations, the living of life according to 'moral' principles which convince people that they are complete in themselves and unconnected to the world outside, has had an enormous *political* effect. Not just on individuals; not just on nations; but on the world.

The life I have been describing is that of a man for whom politics were a dead and repellent duck – but the man I now am feels with passionate conviction from head to bowels that the fact that he could have lived so long like that is a frightening and fearful indictment. Not just an indictment of himself, but of a whole culture. The saxophone player who visited Prague with Colosseum in the closing months of the 1960s had at his disposal the conventional street wisdom of the British tabloids, and nothing at all of any of the following.

In the wake of World War Two the devastated nations of the newly-formed communist bloc faced an urgent need to increase production and raise living standards. In 1962 the USSR, following a Polish suggestion, proposed a planned economy for all the Comecon countries. What the Soviets and the Poles were hoping for was a socialist form of economic internationalism, one which was not contaminated by the various social and political ailments which come with the capitalist version. However, the other Eastern European nations, with Rumania in the forefront, argued forcefully against the idea on grounds of national autonomy; in 1964 the notion was dropped and the various Comecon states proceeded to develop their economies individually, thus becoming involved to varying extents in the ever-present capitalist trade and finance web.

During the mid-sixties, in most Eastern Bloc countries including the USSR itself (though only briefly in 1956–66), the need for increased output in the absence of an overall plan led to a drive towards decentralization and shake-up of the production structures, with, though in varying degrees, the burden of improvement being laid at the point of production rather than at managerial levels. Productivity had to be raised somehow, and the choice was made to lever it up by means of incentive schemes, an emphasis on the right of management to manage, the spread of ever greater pay differentials, and so on. Decisions were no longer made with reference to social equality (the need for the product), but increasingly to profitability (the monetary value of the product – the main capitalist criterion). It was what we in the West might, with a yawn, recognize as a time-honoured ruling-class move. And, as ever, the initiative came from those quarters which would benefit the most in terms of both material goods and power and influence: the managerial and technical strata. Resistance came from the old party bureaucracies with their Bolshevik upbringing and, for obvious reasons, from the bulk of manual workers.

Czechoslovakia was no exception to the general trend. From 1961 to 1968 the real wages of Czech manual workers grew at an exceptionally slow rate, even for a controlled economy. Not so, however, the real wages of managerial and technical personnel. Their salaries increased forty-two per cent faster than those of manual workers. In January 1968, the anti-Bolshevik reforms shifted up a gear with Party First Secretary Novotny's removal from office and replacement by Alexander Dubcek, the Moscow-trained but flexible and liberally-inclined head of the Slovak party. The new government granted managerial autonomy to industrial enterprise managers, further increased the real income of the technocratic 'new middle class' relative to that of manual workers, expanded material incentive schemes (including productivity deals) for manual workers, introduced the managerial right to discharge labour (and thus to create unemployment where there had been none before), and reduced trade-union control. In February 1968, on one of many visits to Prague factories, Novotny told workers: 'If to be a conservative means to oppose the lowering of workers' standards of living, I am proud to be called a conservative.' Not surprisingly, he was vigorously applauded, but no extensive mobilization of workers followed his campaign.

In March the reforms shifted up another gear with the Central Committee Plenum's 'Action Programme', which received – and in turn stimulated – greatly increased support. All the support came, however, from the self-employed and from writers, journalists, the managerial and technocratic intelligentsia, and students – none from manual workers. There were naturally short pay strikes or threats of them. To these demands the reformers responded in the following terms: 'At the present time wages cannot increase until production is made substantially more economic' (Prime Minister Czernik, April 1968).

Since 1965 Czech television had been importing US programmes: 'Jackie Gleason', 'Dinah Shore', 'Doctor Kildare', '97th Precinct' (in 1967 Jon Hiseman – then with Georgie Fame – had played in Prague). In March 1968, state control of the media was abolished, partly as a way of neutralizing Novotny's appeal to the workers. Intellectuals took full advantage, using their opportunities to call into question more and more of the socialist institutions of Czech society. A new level of vocal expression came in the May Day processions, and the Czech reforms proceeded swiftly until, on 20 August, the five nations of the Warsaw Pact sent tanks into Prague, thus abruptly aborting them.

After the Warsaw Pact invasion, the newly-illegal magazine *Student* declared, referring to the Dubcek government's capitulation: 'This is a betrayal not only of ourselves, but also of the historical role assigned to this country: to shake the inhuman structure of Stalinism and to find a human form for socialist order.'

It seems to me that while we ponder on these powerful words, we should also reflect that their argument tells very directly *against* the forces which had intervened, heavy-handed and uninvited, to reverse the galloping impoverishment of the whole Czech working class. I suppose that what the Soviets and the other Warsaw Pact nations saw in Czechoslovakia in 1968 was a classic instance of class struggle flaring up in an unusual location – a centrally-planned socialist economy; a socialist economy where the proletariat, rendered suddenly voiceless and in spectacular disarray by the defection to the other side of the Czech Communist Party, was caught off guard, and was losing hand over fist. I surmise that the question for the Kremlin was this: whether or not national sovereignty could stand in the way of going militarily to the aid of their class allies *within* Comecon. That must have been a new one for them. From before Stalin's time Bolshevik foreign policy had generally shunned military pursuit of class war across national boundaries, often to the despair, confusion and destruction of foreign communists (the fall of the Weimar Republic; the Spanish Civil War). After the Stalin–Churchill 'Spheres of Influence' agreement of 1944–5, no comparable case had arisen – British involvement in the Greek Civil War was in the other sphere. There were eye-witness reports of heavy US troop and tank concentrations on the West German side of the Czech border in the month or so before the Warsaw Pact invasion – if these reports are true, then no doubt that massed presence would have given the matter a sharper edge.

In autumn 1969, just about the time we were playing in Prague, an active rank-and-file movement (which found expression in the Czech Communist Party, and was generally described in the Western press as 'ultra-conservative') grew increasingly impatient with what it saw as the slowness of the measures taken to reverse the reforms of the previous year. Workers mounted a successful campaign against party liberals; the Soviets were reported by the *New York Times* as being concerned lest this movement become too strong and 'Maoist'.

When Colosseum played we were welcomed rapturously, not least, I seem to remember noticing, by the security police who were in attendance. During Jon's drum solo (the structural climax of the entire concert, despite Jon's endearing and enduring disapproval of drum solos), a passage of solo hi-hat – '*mm*-chikka *mm*-chikka *mm*-chikka *mm*-chikka' became extended, and was turned by Jon (who discreetly used his announcement microphone) into a whispered but audible 'Dubcek-a Dubcek-a Dubcek-a Dubcek-a' which permeated the whole large auditorium via the PA system and was, we were later told by our personal manager Colin Richardson, taken up by a sprinkling of the front two or three rows, while most of the audience looked either puzzled and slightly out of their depth, or as though they hadn't noticed. Eventually Jon went on to something else and nothing more was heard of it, despite a certain amount of white-faced panic from Colin. Alexander Dubcek had been replaced by Husak by then; he was about to take up a new appointment as Ambassador to Turkey.

10
'Jon Hiseman's Clothes Museum'
– Dave Greenslade

On 8 November, while we were still away on Clem's first tour, the *Melody Maker* carried a long Bob Dawbarn interview with Jon entitled 'Colosseum 1st birthday – a comment on pop's progression'. He said:

> My main reason for forming the band was that after a year with Graham Bond, six months with Georgie Fame and six months with John Mayall, I was convinced we had not got any bands left as such – plenty of stars with faceless rhythm sections, but no bands. And all the best jazz I ever heard came from bands. The thing that did most to damage jazz was the resident rhythm section with the star soloist. In the same way, Ten Years After are just Alvin Lee and a rhythm section. You also have John Mayall and rhythm section, Jimi Hendrix and a rhythm section. It's difficult to get across to the public this concept of a band. Generally they will only accept one character – like Ian Anderson with Jethro Tull. True, they seemed able to accept the Beatles as such, but even the Bee Gees had their faceless ones in the group. I've tried desperately to get this thing about a band across. I give everybody an equally heavy part in the act, featuring everybody in his own right on the things he does best. The

aim is collective improvisation, a collective whole which is more important than any individual in the group.

When asked if he had got complete satisfaction out of what the group had been doing for the last year, Jon admitted that if he was to be totally honest, the answer was no.

Material is always a problem, and when you are successful it means you are working very hard, and it is difficult to find time to write or even just sit down and think. But I don't want anyone to think I'm not doing what I want to. Every member of the band is playing the result of what he has done before. No one is playing down to an audience to make a living.

Later, Jon observed that

. . . there was the blues boom. The thing that did was to get people used to hearing solos on blues sequences which were almost the same as listening to a good straight melody. That got them ready for the next step. We only play one blues in the act now and the rest is getting more and more complicated, but the audiences are enjoying it . . .

And so it rolled on. We did a hell of a lot of festivals – Bath always worked out an outstanding one. The Plumpton Festival in early August 1970 also seems to have been a high spot judging by the *Melody Maker* write-up. With Yes, Deep Purple and any number of other popular acts on, Colosseum got the main photo and byline 'two of the best solos of the weekend'. But perhaps for me personally the Albert Hall rings a bell; it was the first time I'd made that ornate home of dreadful acoustics when Colosseum supported Steppenwolf, the Stateside progressive rock group I'd met in early 1968 when John Mayall's Bluesbreakers were on the West Coast. The date of our first Albert Hall concert was 2 July 1970.

One exquisite moment that stands out in that season of festivals – at least I think it was that year; I can't be sure – was the Turku Festival in Finland. We wowed the Finns, and afterwards two hip-looking long-haired lads knocked on our caravan door. They seemed a little conspiratorial – furtive almost. We let them in, and only then did they say what had brought them. 'Did we want a turn-on?' they said, and before anyone could say a word, one of them revealed . . . two bottles of whisky.

Another memorable event happened at Fehmarn, the large island to which the north coast of Germany is connected by a road bridge, and from which the Scandinavian sea ferries run. In early September 1970, a group of German promoters decided to run a mammoth pop festival on it, and fell foul of the weather. There were far more groups there than I can remember, but apart from Colosseum there were Alexis Korner, Ginger Baker's Airforce, Sly and the Family Stone and Jimi Hendrix; I have an abiding memory of the moment when a whole lot of musicians were being picked up in a bus from somewhere. Whether it was a hotel or the airport I don't know, but there was a crowd of highly-coloured, garish-looking persons – Hiseman with an enormous head of wild, hip-looking hair and, in total contrast, Hendrix looking calm, quiet and self-contained in a neat light-blue suit. Anyway, it was an ill-fated gig. Starting off cold and grey as iron, the skies started to snow – and kept on. The audience, what we could see of them anyway, were a sea of freezing discontented unhappiness, and who was to blame them? We were all advised not to play, for electrical safety reasons. Alexis was the only one who ignored the advice; everyone else sat in icy caravans until we were taken away and set free. After the gig a rumour circulated to the effect that one of the promoters had waded out into the Baltic Sea and stayed there all night in order to avoid several fates much worse than bankruptcy at the hands of West Germany's Hell's Angels chapters.

There was ill fate of a more serious kind waiting in the wings as well. Less than two weeks later Colosseum's first ever front-of-the-*Melody Maker* spread was swept aside (for ever, as it turned out) by the news that Jimi Hendrix was dead. Before he reached twenty-eight. And shortly afterwards, on 4 October, Janis Joplin died; I had met Janis briefly back in February '68, when John Mayall and the Bluesbreakers had a visit in, I

Cambridge, 1956: a soprano player wondering if he'd like to play tenor

Cambridge Jazz Club, 1959: John Bancroft (p), DHS (ts), Mike Payne (b), Bill Hartnell (d)

Blue Lagoon night club, 1959 – note imperfect embouchure

utlin's, Filey, summer 1958: the Ronnie Smith Quintet with visiting guest star Don
endell making the acquaintance of three unidentified campers

National Youth Jazz Orchestra, Juan-les-Pins, 1960. Some vandal has given DHS a hat and
Mike Vickers (*second right*) a halo

Rehearsing for jazz and poetry gigs, 1961: (*L to R*) DHS, Jeremy Robson, Neil Barton, Spike Milligan

Blues Incorporated, 1962: Alexis Korner (g), Dave Stevens (p), Ginger Baker (d), Cyril Davies (hca), Jack Bruce (b), DHS (ts)

ack Bruce (hca), DHS (ts)

Ginger Baker, 1964

Jack Bruce, 1964

The Graham Bond Organization, publicity shot: (*L to R*) Jon Hiseman, Graham Bond, DHS, Mike Falana

Graham Bond Organization, Marquee, 1963: Jack Bruce (b), DHS (ts), Ginger Baker (d), Graham Bond (org)

Graham Bond, 1964

Graham Bond Organization, Bromley, Kent, 1964

Graham Bond, 1966

DHS

Jon Hiseman attempting to read his morning paper in the Mayall Bluesbreakers' People Wagon, 1968

Bluesbreakers in Manhattan, 1968: (L to R) DHS, Keith Tillman, John Mayall, Chris Mercer

DHS in Colosseum's early days

Colosseum playing short-notice gig at hotel swimming pool, Montreux Festival, 1969: Dave Greenslade (org), Tony Reeves (b), DHS (saxes), Jon Hiseman (d), James Litherland (g)

Late Colosseum publicity shot: (*L to R*) DHS, Chris Farlowe (voc), Dave Clempson (g), Jon Hiseman, Dave Greenslade, Mark Clarke

DHS with Dave Clempson (g)

Clem Clempson looking furtive

Jon Hiseman at Colosseum's Prague concert

Filming, 1970: the one with the non-reflecting head is Mark Clarke

Colosseum in Prague, 1969: (*L to R*) Dave Greenslade, Dave Clempson, DHS, Hungarian friend, Jon Hiseman, Tony Reeves

Germany, 1970: (*L to R*) Dave Greenslade, DHS, Chris Farlowe, Dave Clempson

Neil Ardley rehearsing the New Jazz Orchestra, 1969: (*L to R*) Mike Gibbs (tb), Dave Gelly
(s), unidentified tuba, DHS, unidentified tenor, Barbara Thompson (f, as, ss)

Mike Gibbs with DHS

DHS and son, summer 1972

think, the dressing room in Winterland. She was twenty-seven when she died, too.

At about this time, September 1970, the incredible, the unique Chris Farlowe joined Colosseum. Now we were a six-piece, with on lead vocals a veritable master for whom nothing, no vocal melody line of anybody's invention, was ever difficult to perform – or so it seemed to me. Once he'd got it in there between the ears, he invariably (but I mean *always*) did it with Olympian skill, and with a voice that was second to none. Once he was set free to improvise – a thing which, with every respect to Chris's previous groups, he wasn't often heard doing before he joined Colosseum – he displayed an unexpectedly delightful mastery of the quirky musical ad lib as well.

The band charged on. *Daughter of Time*, the third album, came out in November '70. In that same month we performed a signal service for our very good friends the musical press. Retiring gracefully before Chris Welch, that master of hyperbole – it comes a bit like the Hollywood Superbowl only bigger – I let the *Melody Maker* tell the story.

One of the rewards of the pop life is the 'facility trip'. In this great country of ours, 'payola' is practically unknown. Those who expect pop-up toasters and wine glasses in return for 'certain services' are to be disappointed.

There are, however, occasional bouts of genuine hospitality, with no strings or inverted commas attached.

Last week, I went on such a facility trip to Germany with Colosseum. All expenses were to be paid, including air fares and hotel bills. There was no obligation to write anything about the trip, or the band.

My journey was a kind of thank-you for a recent *MM* feature in which my praise for them had been lavish, nay unstinting. In reviews of their current album and recent performance, there was not even the suspicion of a stint.

Cynics might have been under the impression car loads of gold plate, rich tapestries, valuable paintings and rare first

editions were being delivered to my home. But my remarks were prompted by enthusiasm and my only reward was the satisfaction of a job well done.

Colosseum are one of my favourite groups, and still are – just.

Chris tells us why . . .

Both Colosseum and Free were staying at the hotel, having been on tour together for several days. It soon became apparent that the band were pretty tired of touring, although the gigs had been going well. Colosseum are now most popular with German fans and when we finally got to the evening concert, the youngsters packing the hall were wildly keen and enthusiastic.

Unfortunately Colosseum suffered from a PA fault and voltage drops which hit Dave Greenslade's organ. Thus it was that they played one of their worst sets. It wasn't *all* bad. There were some nice moments from Dick, Chris sang well, and Jon's solo was brilliant by the standards of others, if not his own. Later in a post-mortem laced with some acrimony, the group complained that they could not hear each other, and Jon confided that the sooner he got home the better. This proved difficult as some unknown hands had slashed the tyres of the group's van, and coach. The slogan 'capitalist pigs' had also appeared on the van. Capitalist, hireling 'roadies', tired from a day's exertions licking at the heels of their fascist masters, set about the job of midnight repairs with all the resignation of the bourgeoisie. In the dressing room a young, earnest fan indignantly interrogated the group on their apparently shameless desire to charge money for admission. The name Edgar Broughton was raised and seemed to draw a curious response from the musicians present. Non-capitalist entrepreneurs, operating on strictly Marxist lines, politely offered copies of a bootleg Colosseum album to the group, at the extremely reasonable price of thirty marks. Their anguished manager attempted to explain that the manufacturers of such records were making an immoral and illegal profit, but Jon was quite happy to buy a copy.

Back at the hotel, I was so tired after the superb Nuremberg hospitality that I fell asleep on the bed with my boots on. But this did not help towards a speedy departure in the morning, because the group were ahead of me. They had quit the hotel. Clutching my briefcase with one hand and my head with the other, I peered up and down the street outside the hotel with feelings of mild panic and despair.

'The bastards have gone,' I swore. It was incredible, but true. The calm and wholly unconcerned receptionist agreed that the group, including the manager and roadies, had all checked out. There were no messages, no clues where they had gone or why. It was like the *Marie Celeste* all over again.

'What on earth could I have said last night?' I pondered. Had my description of their set as 'awful' gone beyond the bounds of friendship? There seemed no explanation, and just as I contemplated setting fire to the hotel and throwing myself under a tram, Chris Farlowe appeared. 'That's a bit bad,' he agreed on hearing my plight. 'I'll give 'em a ruck when I catch up with them.' Apparently Chris too had overslept, but was not catching a train to the next gig. He had his car. But this was filled with surplus army equipment, and there wasn't room for a gasmask, let alone a stranded waif.

I have been to swinging New York with Led Zeppelin, the icy mountains of Switzerland with Yes, the deep lakes and pine forests of Sweden with Marmalade, the glamorous casinos of Ostende with Unit Four Plus Two, and the pork abattoir of Cork, Ireland, with the Bonzo Dog Doo Dah Band. But never has a group ditched their scribe with scarcely a mark to buy a crust in a strange city. I felt like a character in a Kafka novel . . .

Jon Hiseman later rang to say it had all been a ghastly mistake.

'I see,' I said coldly.

'What can I do to make it up?' he asked penitently. Not being soured by rancour, it has to be said that there is no wound that cannot be healed by time – and a pop-up toaster and a set of wine glasses.

Chris got the toaster and the glasses by special messenger. I hope they're still in service, Chris.

We worked – up to Christmas, we scarcely came off the road. Then, unusually, half of January and something like a third of February were devoted to rehearsal, and in March we made *Colosseum Live* at a series of UK gigs; the majority of it, as I recall, came from Manchester University on Saturday the 13th.

The mention of the *Live* album prompts me to make a small digression. I want to stand back for a moment and look at the life of the band as a whole. After a running-in period which took us roughly to the beginning of 1969, the band worked smoothly up the lower rungs of the ladder until September or October. That autumn marked the start of a sustained upward shift which lasted for around a year, perhaps a little more. Then we seemed to hit a plateau. The band rode along easily enough; but it travelled on a level, so to speak. It was as if during our third year we were reaping the popularity benefits of our second year's labours while laying the foundations of what was to follow.

Were we resting too much on our critical laurels, I wonder? 'Resting' is scarcely the word – 1971 was as hard-working a year as any. We had fought hard to establish ourselves as a live band, and we'd done that. We'd proved to ourselves as well as to others that a band like ours could be a solid success with audiences – could even on occasion put to shame (almost) the heaviest of the heavy, both in size of audience and in how well we went down. We knew the surge of feeling that comes when a performance has sent thousands home elated and satisfied. But the crucial word is 'live'. On stage we'd fought the best and given a good account of ourselves.

So what I mean by 'resting on our laurels' isn't to do with taking life easily. It's more that having proved ourselves as a live band – we didn't know what to do with it. We had not acquired the knack, if it is a knack, of bringing our recording work up to the same level. We were inclined to think that going down well with large numbers of people, lots of times, was the end of our job, and that album sales were in the hands of others – the Public, a separate and elusive deity whose actions were ultimately unfathomable. Another name for Lady Luck. The Public's buying decisions were beyond understanding and prediction, and therefore beyond control of any sort. I think we basically had little commercial instinct, believing that Good Music (live gigs to happy audiences) was more important and more central to us than Money (album sales). It's not for nothing that in the music world 'product' has come to mean 'recordings'.

To put the matter harshly, we never really cracked studio recording. *Colosseum Live*, as well as being a necessary part of our schedule, and which turned out to be one of the best recordings we made, was also a cop-out and a way of buying time. Live, before an audience, Colosseum always delivered like there was no tomorrow – but on record? And it's not that the albums were anything to be ashamed of, either.

I remember a gig we did on 24 January 1970, at Lanchester Polytechnic in Coventry, with – of all the outrageous things to attempt – the New Jazz Orchestra incorporated in the set, playing Neil Ardley's arrangements to some of our recorded numbers. It was astounding. The hall was packed to the rafters, and the reception we got started off enormous and became gargantuan, utterly incredible. Other bands were on, including Jack Bruce's new group making Jack's post-Cream debut; yet I and the rest of Colosseum had the distinct impression that we wiped the floor with everything in sight.

Another poignant memory is the following. In November 1970 we did a tour with Free in Germany – the same tour about which Chris Welch, he of the pop-up toaster and wine glasses, has written. Free had 'All Right Now' at number one in the charts; the two bands were co-headlining. Before the tour began, however, Free's management understandably demanded that Free close the show. Gentlemen to a fault, we and our management raised no serious objection. A couple of days into the tour, Free, having twice watched half the audience melt away while they were on stage, asked if we could swap round; could they go first? Again, no serious objection. But the trouble was, nine months later we were still hammering round the Netherlands, Germany, Scandinavia, the UK and Italy, with two American tours having fallen through. Free had sold two million albums.

Be that as it may, summer and autumn 1971 was a memorable time. Not only were we big enough to break the attendance record at the Lyceum (on Sunday 15 August) and fill the Royal Albert Hall on our name alone (Sunday 17 October); we also heard, somewhat sceptically as I recall it, that our valiant office's third attempt to set up a second Stateside tour looked like bearing fruit in mid-November.

And not only that, either. We broke up.

On 5 November a sombre band meeting took place in the saloon bar of the pub next to the Dominion, Tottenham Court Road. Jon explained that Clem had had an offer from Steve Marriott, that he wished to accept it, and that in Jon's view he would be a fool not to – that was what he had told Clem. He felt that, rather than struggle at such panic-stricken short notice to find another guitarist of equal stature for the American tour, the band should fold. The assembled personnel took Jon's advice, and we folded.

11
Why Did Colosseum Fall?

On page twenty-five of Peter Frame's *Rock Family Trees*, Volume I, Pete writes:

> Colosseum folded after a festival in Sicily. Dave Clempson: 'The band was losing its impetus and nobody was happy with the way things seemed to be falling apart. Jon wanted to whittle the line-up down to a trio: Mark, him and me – but then the situation came to an abrupt head at this gig in Sicily. I took the trouble to take my own amp on stage and set it up . . . but when we went on, it had gone – and I had to use this awful uncontrollable amp. Jon blamed me for the disastrous sound. I split.'

But Pete Frame's got it wrong. Sorry, Pete. The festival with the guitar sound problem was on 6 September; it had no bearing on the band's break-up two months later. Also, Jon Hiseman claims to have no memory at all of any talk of whittling the band down to three.

The real story is one of a whole lot of chickens coming home to roost at the same time, among them a killer. I shall deal with the killer in more detail later, but first let's look at the rest of the chickens. How's this for a list of circumstances, all coming about during the last week of October and the first few days of November 1971.

One: the third attempt at an American tour, this time with Deep Purple, was subject to two conditions. First: our set should be no more than thirty or at the outside forty minutes long. Second: there should be no drum solo, since Ian Paice (so our office told us) didn't fancy the competition. That meant that none of our most requested numbers could be played unless we lacerated the whole show by playing two or at the most three numbers *and* leaving out the climax.

Two: we had just completed a four-day Scandinavian tour without Chris Farlowe; discussions were under way with a view to replacing him, as it was felt in some quarters that we might have to.

Three: it was time for a new album. We had demo'd four new numbers at Advision Studios, but neither we nor the management were happy with the results. We had no other material in the pipeline.

Four: the Albert Hall concert we'd done on 17 October had received an appalling review from Chris Welch, who said on the strength of it that we had lost our way.

Five: there was also a general feeling that the band was losing its audience.

Six: on top of that lot, in the first days of November Clem visited Jon at his home to say that he'd had an offer of twenty-six thousand pounds, plus the use of a Bentley, to leave Colosseum and play with Steve Marriott. He asked Jon what Jon felt he should do. Jon said he thought he would be mad not to take it, upon which Clem asked what Colosseum would do. Jon, reviewing all the other circumstances in his head, said he doubted if Colosseum would bother to replace Clem at all.

'What does that mean?' said Clem.

'I doubt if the band has a future,' said Jon.

Clem offered to stay on for two months, long enough to see the Stateside tour through, but Jon refused with thanks.

Seven: at the meeting – Jon, me and Dave Greenslade (Chris, Mark and Clem were not present) – no one dissented from Jon's view.

Clem's departure delivered a death blow to a debilitated

creature; yes, it put a weakened competitor out of its misery and out of the race. If it hadn't happened, the band might well have gone on, but it wasn't the real reason. A *healthy* band could have handled something as disastrous as the loss of its lead guitarist with five days to go before a major tour. But then again, perhaps the lead guitarist of a healthy band would not have wished to leave it.

So why was Colosseum a debilitated creature and a weakened competitor? Why wasn't it a healthy band? Why did it finish after a mere thirty-seven months, when the Graham Bond Organization, with just about everything except music weighing the scales against it, worked solidly for four years?

Drug problems? No. Administrative problems, organizational problems, logistical problems, management problems, agency problems? No. Personality clashes? No. Leadership problems? Not really. The decision-making of Colosseum's leader could scarcely have been bettered. The simple truth is that Colosseum was running out of music – and that in a very real, down-to-earth sense. For the previous six months or so we had been finding it more and more difficult to come up with new numbers.

We were running out of music. But it wasn't because our composers were drying up. Dave Greenslade was on the threshold of a most singularly prolific career as a composer. This just adds to the puzzle.

Our lack of music was partly a reflection of the standards we set ourselves. The band was never content with a particular recording format – each album had to be a new kind of entity in its own right.

And the lack of new music was partly because of a sheer shortage of composing time. The band's albums always received a good deal of critical acclaim and had reasonable across-the-counter movement – still going on two decades later – but their sales were not enough to guarantee an income sufficient to allow touring to become what it really ought to be: a non-profit-making advertising exercise. This was the hurdle which the group, had it not died when it did, might well have crossed with the second American tour and the period after it. If we had not had to tour virtually continuously to pay all the various outgoings (wages, management and agency percentages, crew, equipment, upkeep . . .) there would have been more time to compose and rehearse new music and, with that solid background, to design new albums together with their related stage shows.

The problem was also to do with the method the band evolved for producing its music.

The internal structure of virtually anything you care to name, and certainly a rock band, is crucial to its functioning. I want to look at the internal structure of Colosseum for a moment, in order to ask a question about its music.

From the start, Jon Hiseman was the day-to-day administrative leader of the band. No one ever disputed that. He had total support, approval and consent from all of us, not only because he was good at it, but because he was much better than anyone else in the band could have been. Had administrative leadership been the only kind of leadership, the band could have gone on for ever.

In the grey area of musical policy – somewhere between administrative leadership and musical leadership – Jon's solidly established administrative authority leaked across by way of discussion until it dominated, and the vacuum was filled. Jon became by general consent the final arbiter in rehearsals. But in the matter of musical leadership pure and simple, things were different. True musical leadership depends upon being the principal source or fountainhead of the music. If it's a jazz or blues band, it means being the focal point in performance; if it's a progressive rock band, it probably means being the main composer. Jon was (a) not a composer and (b) the drummer. In both of these respects, he was at something of a disadvantage in the role of musical leader.

But no other musical leader arose, and over time Jon's authority leaked from administration to fill the vacuum of musical policy. This wasn't megalomania on Jon's part. It was a team adjusting as best it could to the circumstances it found itself in. Costly rehearsal time had to be used effectively; things had to progress, come what may, for the band to stay alive. New numbers, new music, had to be hammered into shape for performance. I think that at the start Jon expected, or hoped, that he would run the band while someone else ran the music side with him merely as one of the team, and when this didn't happen, he stepped into the breach. He wasn't going to see the beautiful machine he had literally designed, built and put on the road himself splutter to a halt for lack of fuel.

The question has to be asked, though. Given that Dave Greenslade and I were the main writers of the band, how did it come about that we felt we had to get Jon's approval for anything we wanted to do?

Jon and I had a major policy disagreement at the outset. I had very firm ideas about how to build up a repertoire: I felt that we should start from something that we all knew. Starting from a style that was common ground, we should allow the sum of our different ways of playing to develop within the context we all provided for each other, thus letting the band grow as an entity. Each member would be able to express himself musically without deliberately focusing on originality. In this way the band as a whole would not suffer under the stultifying burden of self-consciously trying to do something new. I argued that in the end the result *would* be new, simply because we were who we were, a new combination. Thus the development of the band would be a natural progression rather than the embodiment of some preconceived non-musical goal.

Jon disagreed profoundly with this. He wanted to establish from the start that whatever we were, we were not a blues band. To this end he wanted the direction of the band's style to be consciously controlled. There is, naturally, much to be said on both sides, but one thing that is fairly clear is that the two approaches cannot be happily combined. Jon won the dispute by sheer force of articulacy, and by virtue of his position as prime mover and administrative bandleader. In fact it turned out that Colosseum was in no way a blues band, as our very first number, 'Those About to Die', made quite clear. Be that as it may, Gerry Bron's enthusiasm on hearing what kind of music the nascent band was playing became a forceful argument in favour of Jon's view, and was an important reason why Gerry, as manager, had so much faith in the band throughout its existence. The upshot of all this was that Jon, having first settled the musical-policy argument, found as time went on that he had to go further and become the musical leader as well, simply in order to put his musical policy into effect.

However, Jon's musical leadership was not grounded in the way that his other leadership functions were – in the ability to deliver himself directly, in person. What we had was a number of outstanding players who were also composers of varying ability, range and fruitfulness. We were able to produce pieces – some of which were rejected, some approved, some to become album numbers – that needed very little addition or alteration. As time went on, though, the ideas we worked on became grist to a larger mill. All along, the motor that drove that mill was the idea that Jon and I had hatched way back in the GBO days – the notion of a *band*. A passengerless collective of high-powered equals in which there were no front and rear ranks, no one outstanding figure. As Jon said in his 'first birthday' interview, the aim was to negate the star-plus-faceless-rhythm-section format.

Though Jon was not a composer himself, he had a vision of the kind of music which would express this fundamental aim. He stood over the whole process of musical creation, directing operations, accepting, rejecting, cajoling, doubting, encouraging and criticizing. Piece by piece as the years went by, he watched over the composition of much of the vast architectural music that came to characterize Colosseum, compositions that stood alongside Jack Bruce and Pete Brown's 'Rope Ladder to the Moon' and Mike Gibbs's 'Tanglewood '63'.

The process was rather like a Roman standing precariously astride four horses at once, driving them, guiding them, but not galloping himself. The results at their best had a classic passionate grandeur that was sometimes a surprise to their composers. In a sense it wasn't quite what the composers had composed; it was produced by Jon in something like the way a studio producer produces. And it was magnificent. Colosseum was the innovator of this kind of music – the public could see as well as we could that we *were* all equal, there *were* no passengers and no stars.

In jazz or blues, almost everything depends on the individual performer; the material itself is strictly secondary in the sense that the performer is the star, and the material is there to be bent to his or her will. But if the music is structured and complex, the shape of the music has a big role independently of the performance. Less responsibility thus falls on the performer and more on the composition, and hence on the composer. The ultimate is the classical masterwork, where the composer is almost all there is to be seen musically speaking – the conductor and performers are there to breathe life into grand designs whose smallest detail was settled perhaps two or three centuries ago.

As Colosseum's three years went on, its music became progressively more complex and daringly, demandingly architectural. Now there's nothing wrong with complexity. The most magical bits of music range from the simple to the intricate – in music, complexity has nothing to do with quality. But in the nature of things it takes time and effort to compose structurally complex music. If one of the main driving forces of a group is not himself a composer, but has to resort to words to help get his ideas across, you have a problem, because between music and words there is no direct translation. New, young composing talent may feel inhibited, and the results may turn out to be rather mechanical, because the composition is not a natural development of the music. As Colosseum leapt from album to album, like a traveller crossing a river on stepping stones, it increasingly had to struggle against a tendency towards the contrived and mechanical in its material. The period from the first conception of a piece to its final performance on stage could seem an eternity. Numbers like 'The Pirate's Dream' took six months in rehearsal, being revised over and over again. New ideas seldom stayed simple. By the time they were rehearsed to readiness, they were often almost unrecognizable. I get the same thing now, as a solitary composer – imagine how it was multiplied with three, four or five people involved.

Colosseum never lost the struggle against mechanicalness. On the contrary. It was precisely the effort of winning it every time under unpropitious conditions that cost us so dearly in the flow of new music.

There was something else, too, which had an important part to play in what happened. Increasingly through Colosseum's history, the other members of the band had little idea of what Jon Hiseman had to put up with.

One of the Hiseman dimensions is that of the natural leader of men. He's efficient, a good talker *and* a good listener, he sees what has to be done, and once it's seen he does it. I suspect it's not so much that he likes hard work as that he likes to see a job well done, and in most cases he feels (often rightly) better able to do it than anyone else who's around. Well, one job that has to be done in a band is making decisions.

Another valuable principle of leadership is that decisions should reflect the real thoughts and desires of the people they affect. And here I have to say that I think that everybody in the band except Jon was at fault. We were *not* good talkers. Since then the women's movement has given a lot of practical lessons in speaking one's mind without making enemies as a prelude to working out a collective view. We should have done just that: voiced our opinions on everything from music to management. We hardly ever did.

Even in the smallest of business ventures there's an almost automatic tendency towards the separation of the ruling classes from the workers. You just drift into it. It's really a separation of functions rather than of people. Something of the sort happened in Colosseum. True to our anti-monster anti-nutter tradition, we hit it off from the start as people and continued to do so. We all stayed friends. But as time went by the rest of us got so used to not having to go into the office once a week to talk with management, check the accounts, scan the latest movements on the bookings front and so on, that we were quite happy to sit around and wait for orders. You could say we let it happen. Jon was so obviously good at it, and happy in his role, that there was no point in even trying to change things. After a couple of months Jon was, I'm sure, well aware that if he didn't perform the leadership functions, then like as not nobody else would be able to, let alone want to. I suspect also that there was a part of him that didn't entirely love that situation, but not only was it his creation in the first place – the very success of his efforts guaranteed its continuation.

In among all the excitement, I had been rather impressed with the way Jon had handled things right from the start. It wasn't a joint venture now, this dream of ours, this passengerless nutterless band. It was *Jon's* band, and I was a member of it. The *fait accompli* was complete and irreversible. So for me there was a contradiction from the start. Colosseum was first conceived by Jon and me together when we were with Graham Bond. It had been a challenge to idiot fate, two defiant fingers raised in a cheeky but serious V-sign against an endless landscape of prevailing lunacy. When Colosseum came to birth, however, it was no longer a partnership. It was a team chosen, organized and led from the front by Jon alone. And it was Jon alone who had decided that it should be this way.

In their armoury of concepts, social psychologists have a useful-looking weapon called cognitive dissonance. Cognitive dissonance is supposed to have among its effects a clouding of the subject's understanding of what is happening in himself, and consequently leads to a certain shortfall in sorting out the causes. Throughout the life of Colosseum, I obstinately continued to feel two opposed and unreconciled things: one, that Colosseum was a baby that Jon and I had conceived and nurtured together; two, that Colosseum was Jon's baby and not mine at all.

Colosseum both was and was not the band I had cherished the thought of. I never did sort this out at the time; I wasn't really aware of it. But I do have a very distinct memory of an incident around the end of October or beginning of November 1968, shortly after the band had started its working life. Jon and I were driving through the various Twickenham roundabouts on the A 316, me the passenger in Jon's car. As he drove, Jon told me quietly and seriously that he needed me to take a more positive role in the organizational side. He felt disappointed that I had not done so spontaneously. I felt awkward; I didn't want to hear it. I think I said something about needing my time for my private life. But that wasn't the real issue between Jon and me, however heavy my private life – or his, come to that. The real issue was how the band had come into existence. I felt then – and still feel now, only more articulately – that ideas are not enough, words are not enough; only actual material existence determines. The way the band had been born made it his, not ours. Now maybe Jon would have disagreed with this, maybe he would have thought quite differently, or maybe he would have argued and had something revolutionary to add. My point is, though, that we don't know what could have been said. Whatever we thought and felt, the pair of us, remained unknown because it was not discussed. The discussion could, and should, have confronted the matter. If it had, maybe the history of Colosseum could have been longer. But no discussion took place. Instead I turned him down, and saddened, he said no more about it.

So. My End of Colosseum Theory adds up to this. A number of circumstances combined to render the band vulnerable.

(a) We were running out of new music because we set ourselves high standards; there was a chronic shortage of composing time due to our record sales having consistently failed to exceed the initial advances, meaning we had to tour almost continuously to pay our way; and the way Colosseum composed and rehearsed tended to take up a good deal of time and effort anyway.

(b) Jon was tired, isolated and lonely in his leadership role, especially with the other problems that had cropped up.

(c) At the crucial moment, just before a major tour, Clem's Steve Marriott offer came up and he wanted to take it.

The weight of all these things happening together combined suddenly to stop Colosseum in its tracks.

To me the most puzzling feature of Colosseum's short history is this: in the whole thirty-seven months, no real musical leader, no true composer or composing team in the usual sense of the words, rose to dominate the music of Colosseum. Why did Jon have to shoulder the responsibility of a job for which he was not really qualified, and continue to carry it? It's always seemed to me that Hiseman at his most inspired – classic Hiseman – is Hiseman caught short and responding with his instincts before his formidable mind has a chance to catch up. That is, Hiseman working with somebody else's music, and in the process transforming and enlarging it, highlighting its strengths. As I've said, for me Jon is the arch-responder, not the initiator. His drumming is the lush, fruitful backcloth, not the subject in the foreground. His early closeness to the style of Elvin Jones of the John Coltrane Quartet helped greatly to form him in this mould. Perhaps the Colosseum Jon hoped would emerge of its own volition – but which as it turned out did not emerge – would have played Coltrane to his Elvin. Jon Hiseman would be the one to tell us that.

Well, there's always the Lap of the Gods Theory. The moment Colosseum's direction began to establish itself, it already had on it the stamp of its own peculiar origins, in which Jon's role as producer rather than responder played a large part – it would have taken a mature composer or a steamroller to alter that. In other words, once Jon had taken on the role of musical director, the success that he and the band enjoyed ensured that he must continue in that role, even if it meant limiting the life of the band.

12
A Story Ended

The news of Colosseum's break-up hit me in the form of a phone call that Guy Fawkes morning. I guess I knew it was coming: a warning from the gut.

And so it was. It was as if the decision had already been taken. 'Motion carried brothers. Thank you very much.' I walked out of the meeting that evening feeling as though it had all happened before, many times.

Grim thoughts. 'OK, so I can survive this one too, right?'

Sometimes the confirmation of a foreboding is worse than a bolt from the blue.

Six days later, on Thursday the 11th, C— and I went to the Royal Albert Hall to hear Bach's B Minor Mass. The performance was splendid; the auditorium half-empty. For Colosseum, three weeks and four days earlier – unknowingly playing our last concert – it had been not just full but packed to the rafters, heaving. Even, unfortunately for Colosseum, some damage had been done to the seating; enough for Bron's to receive a bill.

During the performance I pondered. For the moment, and not without relief, I ceased to think about my own future. In my book the B Minor Mass is music without compare. C—

observed that Bach had died two hundred years ago, and that his work was still being performed as much as ever, if not more. Colosseum had existed for three years, not two centuries ago but now. It had ceased to exist, which meant that its music would never be performed again, yet it had pulled twice the audience that had come to listen to Bach. I heard what C— said. I drew no conclusions. I just allowed those thoughts to sink in as the music roared and danced and floated majestically through me.

The next year and a half was an unsettling time for me. If I am honest, looking back on that period is one bloody great frown. I could sum it up by saying that for me as a musician, everything worked all right and nothing worked well. With hindsight, though, I have to admit that the source of the problem was not to be found outside of me. Up to then I had always operated by discovering some standpoint from which my situation, whatever it was, could be enjoyed. For the first time, that stratagem failed. I was no longer free to search for a standpoint. The one I *had* to take – that of bandleader and boss – was one from which my situation simply could not be enjoyed. But more of this navel-observation later; first let me give an outline of the sequence of events.

Gerry Bron, eager for a new band to arise out of the bones of Colosseum, made it clear that he would stand by to help in any way he could. I took it step by step. The obvious and logical thing to do was to raid some of the material that lay half-completed to make an album of my own. That I did, first making contact with Pete Brown, the poet/lyricist with whom I'd worked in the fifties and early sixties in the New Departures-sponsored jazz'n'poetry gigs, and who had recently been Jack Bruce's co-worker on a lot of Cream numbers. Pete and I worked on my stuff until we were reasonably satisfied, ready at least to get it into the stage of rehearsal. I also contacted Jon Hiseman; Jon wrote lyrics to a blues I'd written for which, typically, I had a title but no words. Finally I had more than enough material to be sure of being able to put an album together. The next thing was to settle on the personnel.

I shopped around. Eventually I decided to divide the album into two, the first half basically music that had come from Pete and me; the second half music which reflected the co-operation between myself and Jon. I also settled on Jon as the producer of the album, not least because the *magnum opus* on it was going to be a leftover from Colosseum, 'The Pirate's Dream'. That was a composition of mine, Dave Clempson's and Jon's that had started life as a twinkle in Jon's eye called 'Let's Do a Number that Hasn't Got Any Solos in It'. It had gradually grown until it became a twelve-minute epic albatross that hung around Colosseum's neck – even, in its way, playing a minor role in its demise. Colosseum had performed it with its heart in its mouth quite a few times, including once on a BBC broadcast that I for one would be interested to hear, but it had never had the brass neck to play it in a studio.

Various people have done me the honour of imagining that the title of the album, *A Story Ended*, signified that I somehow knew I was going to leave music entirely two years later. It's a nice thought, but unfortunately it's fantasy. I just liked that particular Eliot quote, and for no very clear reason wanted to see it on the cover. I remember that I knew that before I knew almost anything else about the album.

The way I went about it was definitely material-based. I invited particular musicians whose work I liked and respected to come and play on numbers I hoped they'd feel at home on. Paul Williams on vocals, Caleb Quaye on guitars, Mark Clarke (bass and vocals), Dave Greenslade (keyboards), Chris Farlowe (vocals) – these last three from Colosseum – Rob Tait on drums. Jon, who played drums on 'The Pirate's Dream', Chris Spedding on guitar, Gordon Beck on piano and Graham Bond on keyboards and vocals completed my guest list at the young Richard Branson's Manor Studios in Oxfordshire. The whole thing took, if I recollect aright, two lots of five days spanning the end of March and the beginning of April 1972. It was hard work, but I must admit I enjoyed it a lot.

After we'd finally got everything in the can and mixed, and Jon and I had cut it at Apple, off it went to Gerry's Bronze Records. In fairly short order, out it came. It got reasonable reviews, and meanwhile I occupied myself in putting together a road band. The first thing I did was make contact with James Litherland, Colosseum's first guitarist/singer. It turned out that he already had the making of a band – or rather it wasn't just the makings, it was the guitar–bass–drums trio and it was pretty damned good. Billy Smith was on bass, John Dentith (Theodore Thunder) on drums, and they all sang. We talked, played, decided on a link-up; advertised for a keyboard player. Pretty quick we had him: Dave Rose. We settled on rehearsal time and places, and I took a short holiday with C— before we began in earnest. I was a bandleader.

It was now August 1972, and things were moving fast. We rehearsed in August and September, and in October we were trying the band out before audiences on a short run-in in Germany. A few gigs in the UK, and there we were – unbelievably – en route to the States, to do a six-week tour third on the bill to Deep Purple and Fleetwood Mac. A new band could scarcely have had a better send-off. But something obscure was wrong . . .

I was unhappy. I felt at one remove from everything.

The reason was that I was in control, and I didn't want to be. Why didn't I want to be in control? It wasn't that I didn't like being a bandleader, or that I couldn't handle the responsibility. It was deeper than that, so deep that I wasn't really aware of it. I was beginning to question the entire scheme of things whereby one person controls many. These questionings and others like them surfaced later with devastating and joyous consequences for me. Then they weren't even conscious.

I chose the word 'questionings' carefully. I didn't reject the idea of leadership; I just hadn't positively accepted it because I hadn't considered the matter. But as I found myself propelled for the first time into the role of a leader, something in me realized that the act of becoming a leader in itself presumed a positive commitment in favour of one-person-in-control-of-many. No such commitment had been made.

It's OK to be a follower – a sideman – because the commitment is negative. You don't have to do anything except just play. In a sense, as a sideman you are let off the hook of having to decide about anything. If, like me, you had dismissed the whole thing as tiresomely theoretical and irrelevant, being placed suddenly in the leadership position gives things an uncomfortable jagged edge which makes the issue very immediate. When I did start to think about it, it very rapidly became apparent that I had committed myself politically to a position I could not support: being the leader of an organization.

Typically, though, I ignored the whole bloody issue of why I wasn't feeling too good as a bandleader, and got on with the job, dimly aware that I was taking the first steps towards becoming either a monster or a wreck, or possibly both at once. I became more and more dictatorial. As my cassette collection shows, the band had been playing consistently well – beautifully in fact – all along. From the first few gigs before the American tour it had been funkier, solider, more and more exciting. It was a Get Down band, slightly Tower of Power-ish, slightly Average White Band-ish. I should have been happy, but I wasn't. For no reason that I could discern, I felt that silly, shifting discomfort with my surroundings that people like me label 'weird'. In Chicago I hired a huge American station wagon and drove round like a character in a B movie, getting the standard vicarious sense of freedom and anonymity. I drove down to the South Side, went to see Eddie Jackson, whom I hadn't seen for years. We talked; it was a relief to see him. Apart from many personal things that occupied us, it was good to see someone I was close to who knew me only from the days before I was on the road. But I wasn't able to talk about the way I was feeling, not even with him, I wasn't. The thing that was bothering me wasn't ripe for discussion. I think the nearest I got to it was some brief and awkwardly light-hearted rubbish about being a bossman now.

And so onwards, coast to coast. Then home.

After the Purple tour was over, back in the UK in December '72 and January '73, I began to feel that our management situation wasn't all it could be. After discussing it with Gerry, I made contact with another management organization. Eventually Gerry and I wound up our working association amicably by mutual agreement, and I was with a new manager and agency with whom I hoped I would see eye to eye, especially on the subject of a new album. The first thing I wanted to do was get into the studios. There was plenty of new material floating happily out of all of us – Billy, John, Dave, James and myself. We set about rehearsing it, and lo! next thing, we were in Escape Studios, a small but highly serviceable sixteen-track in Kent. The tracks went down, a whole album's worth. We left the sax parts till the end . . .

Meanwhile my old slipped disc was giving trouble. I ignored it: the Show Must Go On. The show went on. The back got worse. I gritted my teeth heroically and ignored it: the Show Must *Absolutely* Go On!

One morning around the end of April 1973 I got up in West Hampstead, had breakfast, went out en route for the car and the Kent studios where we were due to put down the sax parts and start mixing, took the first two steps down the four flights to ground level – and realized then and there that I wasn't going anywhere. Gradually I moved very gingerly back to the door of the flat. C— let me in, horrified, and called the doctor while I lay on the bed groaning and sweating, howling and grunting. My fifth lumbar disc had well and truly done what it had been threatening to do – split in a gross rupture. The jelly-like substance inside the disc was squirting out and hitting my sciatic nerve with every breath and twitch. Movement – any movement whatsoever – was horrific. It was more than just painful.

And that was the way it stayed. Art Themen, by then an orthopaedic surgeon, came to see me PDQ, took one look, and said, 'Right. Off the bed, on the floor. Stay there on your back until it gets better. Then keep staying there. That's it. It'll get better if you let it, not if you don't.' The authoritative tone was complete and undoubted.

And that, bar the shouting, was the end of my band.

Looking back now, I can see that after Colosseum I did all the things that were logically the obvious things to do: making my solo album, forming my own working band, taking on the decision-making responsibilities and so on. But I was doing the whole thing sleep-walking. I was doing the logical things because they were the logical things to do, not because I wanted to do them. It was as if I were doing it back to front, assuming that because it was logical then I must therefore want to do it.

The fact is that my main connection with music is through playing. Writing it, listening to it, talking about it are all secondary. If I don't play, my interest in music dries up, and the curious thing is that bandleading seemed to relegate playing to a very low priority.

I had somehow mislaid music along the way, in two ways. As a bandleader, I was focusing less and less on my playing; and at the same time the 'rhythm', as it was, of my life was changing underneath me in ways for which I was not prepared.

During the months of painful enforced idleness on the floor of the flat in West Hampstead I was spending more and more time *thinking* – an occupation I found strange and difficult, as if I were using creaky muscles I never even knew I possessed. I wasn't thinking too well yet, but so what? A baby doesn't walk too well. You need tools to think, and I had only toys.

I thought about things I had had little time for until then, all the standard pulpy stuff pondered upon by the bewildered: What is Wrong with the World? Why is there So Much Violence? Is Human Nature Bad? I began to dream, too, of having another life, another profession entirely, perhaps one in which C— and I could take off into the wilderness in a Range Rover and make exciting paleoanthropological dis-coveries.

I began to feel a profound resentment towards all the countless strident, confident voices of political and intellectual opinion with which the air was filled – had been filled all my life, so it appeared. There were disagreements on all sides, and yet every single disputant seemed utterly cocksure that his or her own view was *right*. Time after time those who prevailed did so because they were more articulate and better able to impose their own view as *authoritative*. That was all it required. Those who could shout best won.

It was that utter confidence that got my goat, because if two people disagreed then it must be obvious to the dimmest lowbrow ignoramus – even to me lying on the floor – that they might both be wrong, or that one might be wrong and the other right, but what was for absolute certain sure was that they couldn't both be right.

I deeply resented the sheer arrogance with which talking heads of all stripes seemed to expect me and millions like me, ignoramuses all, to accept what they said just because *they* said it. To ask for evidence, be it never so humbly, was an occasion for sneers. To ask to hear an opposing view put with conviction was tantamount to treason.

Like a lot of musicians, I had always been sceptical of politics in general, but to be frank I hadn't attached enough importance to it to bother with it. Now I began to feel that many of the questions which politics verged on in its own peculiar distorted way were profoundly important, and my scepticism increased a thousandfold. It became a matter of fiery anger, an anger based as I knew only too well on having a bloody great vacuum of ignorance where basic, simple, useful, down-to-earth factual knowledge – rather than opinion – ought to be. A vacuum filled with hearsay and myth and cosy self-satisfied beliefs held only in order to help the holder feel more comfortable and at home in the world.

In short, I came face to face with my own intellectual bankruptcy, and shortly after that I realized that I had only one reliable ally in my paltry armoury of thought-aids: my scepticism. It was the one tool I needed to make merciless war on comfortable lies.

I tried to formulate my thoughts on paper. I even remember a strange little one-page effort at analysing what was wrong with the world in terms of some basic defect in human nature.

Eventually I got humbly in touch with an old friend of mine, Paul Hebden, who I knew was some sort of lecturer somewhere, though I didn't know what he was a lecturer in. Paul came over and sat on a chair beside my pallet-on-the-floor and grilled me for an hour or so. He talked to me like a dutch uncle (whatever that means) and eventually gave forth the opinion that I might make a fair social-science student if I really wanted to work hard, though getting a grant was another matter. He told me to think about it carefully, and not to imagine that it would be any kind of soft option. He concluded with a warning not to enrol at his own Polytechnic of the South Bank, as I'd have a better chance going somewhere where I didn't know anybody. He recommended that I read a couple of slim introductory volumes to see if social-science textbooks were my cup of tea.

Eventually, round about the end of August or so, I was able to stand up. I had no cash and nothing in the bank. Throughout my whole career in music, not one of the bands I had ever been with had done more than pay the wages – not even Colosseum, with the exception of one two-thousand-pound bonus. So I went round to a local minicab firm and hired myself and my car to it for three weeks. The good old music profession did me proud there, I must say: the only piece of news about me since Colosseum ended was that I was driving a taxi! That's come back to me lots of times since then. Oddly enough, during my three weeks one of my fares was Marianne Faithfull. I kept my head down and escaped without being recognized, though she probably wouldn't have known who I was anyway.

And the next thing was that I was queueing up to sign into the foundation year of a BSc (Soc. Sci.) at – yes, you've guessed it – the Polytechnic of the South Bank. The saxophone went into its case and did not come out again for three solid years.

Afterword:
Race and Racism in Music

I

The last few years has seen the emergence of a generation of British-born blacks, complete with local accents – and you'd be surprised what a difference that makes – in numbers sufficient to make them a significant and active sociopolitical and cultural force. As a result, for the first time ever a high proportion of fresh jazz talent in the UK is black. Not surprisingly, race and racism is on the agenda.

By and large, though, nobody wants to talk about it in a serious, reasoned, hard-hitting way, except from the safety of a media outlet. Racists regard people with skins of a different colour than their own as unwelcome presences, to be either ignored or else positively, but subtly, shut out. Liberals regard racism itself as an unwelcome presence and prefer to ignore it wherever possible; sometimes – and this is a particularly tortuous effect of racism – people seem almost embarrassed to discuss racism with people who have different skin colour from their own. And then there are the countless millions of practical-minded innocents who say, 'I'm not a racialist of course. But between you and me, to be honest I don't really trust them,' or some such thing. (As if one only becomes a racist by explicitly adopting racism as a theoretical position, rather than racism *appearing*, as it were, of its own volition in a collection of practical actions over time.) The result of all this is that racism lives on unlabelled, unidentified, unmolested and as strong as a horse, at the heart of Western culture. In any case, right at the bottom what we call racism is not without its own causes. Underneath racism, and in turn disguised by it, lie the power relations that arise from a lengthy history of economic inequality.

Until recently – the last decade or so, I guess – I've ignored racism almost completely. If called upon to say something about it twenty years ago, I'd probably have said something like, 'we don't have any of that in music' and then dried up; I thought it so inexplicable and irrelevant that I just didn't want even to think about it. If forced to say what I really thought I'd have said it was some kind of crackpot mania affecting a tiny, repellent and basically certifiable minority. I wouldn't have said it was a particularly British phenomenon, either: much more American than British, I'd have said, then.

I don't plan to write a tract on racism, not in this book at least. What I'm going to do is try to tell my own story on the role of race and racism in jazz; and to this end, the species of racism I'll be talking about is exclusively black/white racism. I'm well aware that there are others, naturally, but they don't seem to me to be particularly germane in the present context.

As far as I know, I'm about as white as you can get.* The first black person I ever met was a kid at school, by name Kaye Dunham. He was the nephew of Katherine Dunham the dancer, but at fifteen I had more than enough on my plate without worrying about the significance of other people being related to world-famous dancers. Kaye turned out to be quite significant in himself, as far as I was concerned.

One of the things on my plate was music. At my previous school I'd had the beginnings of classical clarinet for a year or so, and I'd acquired two ten-inch 78s: Benny Goodman's 'Bach

*And incidentally, if it's true (as the latest genetic evidence tells us), that the entire human race – every human being on this planet – is descended from one African woman who lived about four million years ago, then whatever happened to my black skin? Or was she brown? And what the hell does it matter anyway?

Goes to Town' and Pee Wee Hunt's '12th Street Rag', both of which I played into the ground. Somehow I'd managed to persuade my father to get me a £25 alto saxophone – Boosey & Hawkes – which I played a lot, especially after I discovered the gorgeous alto bits in Dohnanyi's 'Hary Janos' Suite and Ravel's sumptuous orchestration of Mussorgsky's 'Pictures at an Exhibition'.

When I arrived at Dartington there were only two things I liked: farms (cows and tractors in particular) and music; everything else, including people, I feared and loathed. So naturally one of the first things I did off my own bat was hover on the outskirts of the boogie-woogie jam sessions that were being indulged in by some of the kids under the *loco-parentis*-type wing of a teacher, Robin Johnson, who played a lot of piano. I'd never had any instruction in jazz. I'd never blown with anyone, for the simple reason that there was never anyone to blow with. I hadn't a clue about chord sequences or any intricate, mysterious things like that; I didn't even know they existed. All I could do – and all I wanted to do! – was blow with that sound, that living sound, and go with that rhythm. Nobody told me any different, so I did, tentatively, when I thought it sounded all right; and it was delicious. Robin Johnson spoke gently to me afterwards, pipe in mouth, about keys, chords and so forth; he explained some things, and I was able to try them. I tried them again the next time, and it worked a treat. It was easy once you got the picture, and it made playing ten times more delicious. I went on hanging around the jam sessions, trying things out, and still nobody bothered me. It was a good school that way.

Then Kaye (who also played clarinet at the jam sessions) approached me looking tall, forbidding and at least sixteen. I was nervous. I had no need to be. All he did was quietly and warmly make friends, saying that he liked my playing and that I was a much better clarinet player than he was, and then proceed rather forcefully – but still warmly – to insist that I must bring my clarinet to the end music room. Some of the boys were having, he said with a sparkle of anticipation, a jazz session. He marched off; I followed him. He made sure I did.

I can still remember it. In that close, foetid atmosphere, the little odd-shaped room seemed somehow purified by noise. I played. Kaye played. The trumpet player played. The trombone player played (he was Niall O'Casey, Sean's younger son). The piano player played. The drummer played. The bass player played. Not 'Bach Goes to Town' nor '12th Street Rag'; 'Muskrat Ramble', 'Tiger Rag', 'Beale Street Blues', 'Wild Man Blues', 'Royal Garden Blues' . . .

And so on. I learned quickly, with the brightness of sheer delight. Weeks passed. Kaye, who was technically not right for the clarinet but had a great feel, seemed gradually to drop out of playing. He hung around a lot though, a smiling presence, and listened and was pleased. It was as if I was a credit to him: as if, without either asking for or getting any advice, I was doing for real what he, not I, had known all along I *could* do. I didn't think about it. I was happy; I became stronger fast, for one simple reason: I was doing something I *wanted* to do. Something was coming out of me that was in there from long before I was born.

Then one day I heard Sidney Bechet play 'Bechet's Creole Blues'. (I don't remember for sure that it was on the BBC, but I guess it must have been. Anyway I remember reading a printed listing of the recording somewhere.) I wrote instantly to a London record retailer, experienced a century-long week of crazed deprivation, and (at last!) owned it, along with another seven Esquire sides of Bechet with Claude Luter's band.

That did it. I went to Plymouth, found a £10 Maltese soprano saxophone, and 'persuaded' my long-suffering and impecunious father to buy it. I spent rapturously ardent, sweaty days discovering in precise, microscopic detail exactly what Bechet had played in that studio, and exactly how he'd played it. *Exactly*. Know what I mean? *Exactly*.

This music *meant*, with white-hot, burning accuracy, more than any other music I'd ever heard – and what it meant was what I had meant all along. It was not a matter of balanced judgement, of argument and consideration. The subject was suddenly closed, the debate had ended for ever in total, serene accord between me and myself. I *knew*. And looking back on it it's a good thing I did, because the rest of my life was about to detonate thunderously, to shatter and descend into a three-year abyss. Does anybody – do *you*? – remember what it's like being fifteen?

Kaye left the school some time during my first year; that is, in 1950. He must have been sixteen or seventeen, and I guess he went back to the United States. It was years before it dawned on me just what, possibly, he was going back to. I would be pretty happy to meet him again, forty years later.

II

Each venture is a new beginning, a raid on the inarticulate with shabby equipment always deteriorating in the general mess of imprecision of feeling, undisciplined squads of emotion.

T.S. Eliot, *The Four Quartets*

Throughout my life as a jazz musician I've had people – mostly white, come to think of it, but not always – come up to me and pay me the compliment of saying I play like a black. They're always utterly sincere: there are no strings attached, no ifs or buts. Mostly I take it as it's meant, as a simple, high compliment. Occasionally, though, I reflect on it. Once, dripping with sweat and struggling to get two saxophones and a sax stand safely through a sardine-packed and wildly excited crowd, I barked, 'No I don't, I play like a white, OK?' or some such thing. I regretted it instantly. It was crude and brutal and totally uncalled-for, and all it did was hurt the poor well-meaning bloke who had said I played like a black. His face crumpled up before my eyes; he even looked scared for a second or so.

It's a most peculiar thing though, when you think about it. What's really being said is, 'You play *as well as* a black.' The first thing you feel is 'Ooh! That's nice!' Then comes the Daffy Duck sideways retake: 'Hold on – what the hell is this? I'm some kind of a counterfeit or something? Such a good copy even an expert can't tell the difference?' Underneath it all is a racial stereotype: you're supposed to be pleased to be told you have a very close resemblance to something that you're not. Does Jessye Norman get told she sings like a white, I wonder? What would be the response? Is classical music White Music?

To make matters even more confused I am warmed by this particular compliment, even though it can sometimes jar. I know just exactly what it means. The musicians I like all 'play like a black'. Armstrong, Bechet, Johnny Dodds, Pee Wee Russell, Eddie Barefield, Lester Young, Wardell Gray, Muddy Waters, Wolf, T-Bone, Charlie Parker, Sonny Rollins, Elvin Jones, John Coltrane, Lee Morgan, Wayne Shorter, Steve Cropper, Albert King, David Sanborn . . . But is it a particular way of playing, a particular kind of music? Or is it race?

The other day I saw a TV programme about the current British jazz scene; its main focus was Courtney Pine, as a sort of emblem of the upsurge of black talent in the UK. It included some clips of George Melly, commenting on jazz in the UK in the immediately post-war period when I was still at school.

'Well, we couldn't exactly change the pigment of our skin,' laughed George, face crinkling with manic humour: a wickedly intelligent gnome speaking truths from within the comfort of a check suit. The absurdity of it suddenly washed out of the screen, submerging me in oblique mirth. Jesus!

It's a pity George didn't expand a little; maybe he did and there wasn't room for it in the edit. What the discussion omitted to mention was that if that 'we' of his *had* developed black skins, it wouldn't have changed a thing. The colour of your skin is not what it is a matter of. It's what that colour tells you, that's what it's a matter of. Your history, your family's history, *their* families' histories, your culture's history, back for millennia after millennia. Time goes, for ever, down a one-way street! Use all the plastic surgery, make-up, costume devices and so on that you can devise – there's no altering the past. The only thing that isn't actually debarred is altering the future.

This little tale illustrates the yawning gulf between what people think they are doing and what they are actually doing.

George, quite rightly I think, says that the (mainly middle-class and occasionally working-class) white UK jazzers of the late forties and the fifties – those who were not modernists, at least – worshipped North American black musicians of twenty to thirty years before, tended to dismiss North American whites of the same vintage, with the occasional exception of Bix Beiderbecke, and wished above all to *be* black; as a result, they took the only road open to them and tried to play black music. I agree. In my way, I was one of them for a short while – witness my little bit of schooldays autobiography a few pages back – except that I hadn't attached the subtleties of skin colour to those of music; what got to me was, specifically, contemporary Sidney Bechet, and blues; I didn't care one way or the other what colour people were. (Also I have to say that I shifted out of copying styles, more or less when I made the transition to modern jazz.) No names no pack-drill, but there were some who, I suspect, thought they'd actually become black inside (if not out) by some sort of musical osmosis . . .

But what that huge, amorphous 'we' of George's was actually doing was something quite different. Nothing wrong with that; helping to establish revivalism is not a wholly unworthy thing to be remembered for, I suppose.

I'm not a professional historian so I stand to be corrected by those who know better. But, briefly, here is the essence of what I've gathered about the beginnings of jazz; or rather, of the enormous corpus of music – a thousand and one different styles – which for the moment, and for convenience, I call jazz.

First: without exception all its original producers were of African descent but were not Africans.* They were all either

---

*Here I deliberately employ the racists' concept of black, where genetically speaking 'white' means '100% European' and 'black' means 'not 100% European'. It is almost certainly true, given the *droit de seigneur* of slave-owners, that some of the originators of jazz were of mixed parentage – 'octoroons', or whatever. But they were socially classified as black, and they suffered all the associated disadvantages. My intention is, precisely, to make the racists eat their own words and understand the bitter taste of them.

Racists can't suddenly reverse the situation when it suits them. That is, slaves, ex-slaves, or the descendants of slaves imported from Africa, and all were born and bred in one culturally unified area and period, the South of the United States of America after the Civil War: they were Black Americans from the South. Southern whites, Northern blacks and Northern whites learned from their music, which spread as part of their baggage when they moved North in search of work and opportunities for themselves and their descendants.

Second: the musical materials – the traditions – from which they forged this new-thing-on-the-face-of-the-earth were three in number. They were: African song and rhythms, together with the huge and complex social significance song and rhythm carry in African societies; European popular religious music, i.e. to a large extent *Hymns Ancient and Modern*; and European popular secular music, notably brass-band marches and string-band dance music. Also very significant was the fact that these originals had little or no money and hence no access to sophisticated technical resources; mostly they had to use what they could pick up here and there in the way of instruments, or else make them; in short, for the most part they had to find new ways of playing instruments that were not designed to do the job. All these things – mixed together by the astonishing creative forces that the human race embodies, and upon which, apparently, it is always able to call in conditions of adversity – went into the crucible from which jazz emerged like a hitherto unknown compound suddenly appearing, where before there had been nothing but ordinary and well-known chemicals. To summarize: jazz is not African, except in the important sense that all its first practitioners were of African descent; neither is it European. It is American. But this fact tells us less and less with every day that passes, for such is its power that it is increasingly international.

---

they cannot start claiming a white share in the creation of something that is now considered admirable and accepted, like jazz, just because of the possibility that some of jazz's original creators were disowned by their white forefathers. If the racists said they were black *then*, then by god they stay black *now*.

So am I forever condemned to inauthenticity as a jazz-stroke-blues-stroke-whatever musician by the colour of my skin? That is, by my culture's history, of which my skin stands as an indelible sign? It sometimes seems that to label jazz Black Music is to say precisely that. It's a dangerous area, because it almost says, along with the NF, that race is fundamental; absolutely in command. If race *is* in command, then every time I go on to the stand I am part of no tradition whatever; I have no history; I represent no cultural voice. Unlike white classical musicians and black jazz musicians I have nothing and no one behind me, I represent nothing and no one but myself; I have no bank-roll of authenticity to draw upon but am forever on square one fighting for a place. To reduce this to its ultimate racist absurdity: if I play well it is because I've learned to copy a music that is intrinsically not my own; and if I play badly, well then it's not surprising because I am white and it's no more than is to be expected – literally, a Pale Imitation.

Back to George and his pigment for a moment. Wanting to change the colour of your skin is an odd desire, and the more you think about it the odder it gets – always assuming that you're white to start with. At first sight it looks a bit like the US pre-Black Power blacks' wanting to pass for white; but on second glance it's very different. The reasons for trying to pass for white were cruelly practical: if it worked, doors were opened that were simply not an option for blacks. There's nothing remotely comparable, life-opportunity-wise, in trying to pass for black.

So what was it all about, if it wasn't really about skin colour? A symptom of a culture trying to tear itself free of brain-dead musical traditions?

III

I start from one single premiss: that racism is a white problem and not a black one.

I mean this, not in the sense that it's not a problem for blacks (obviously), or in the possibly true but not quite relevant sense that it's a 'psychological' problem for whites, but in this sense: that *you* cannot recover from *my* cold.

Racism is a white problem for one reason. To be quite blunt: the slave trade.

It was Europe and Europe alone that turned the ancient and horrific practice of slavery into a genuine industry: a full-time profession peopled with dynamic, ambitious entrepreneurs whose achievement was to make plentiful, and thoroughly re-investible, profits out of buying and selling live human beings as a bulk item in the international commodity markets of the time.

Europeans are white. The collective responsibility for this hard-to-contemplate gargantuan atrocity falls, therefore, squarely on white shoulders. Let us hear no more of grasping African chiefs; they were not entrepreneurs but tradition-bound despots.

My argument, though, is not at all that any particular whites are (or should be) crazed with guilt. My argument is that European culture as a whole has a particular, *cultural*, disease; it is a disease called racism; and it was brought on by the slave trade in particular.

So I am suggesting that it is the culture that is racist, not individual people. I'd go further and say that we human beings, whatever our views – i.e. racist or otherwise – are not so much the victims of this disease as its carriers; when an anti-racist, just as much as a racist, expresses his or her views it is the sickness of the culture that is being expressed.

This seems to me to have the ring of truth. It makes sense, for instance, of the weird circumstances that anti-racists such as myself (and, I presume, Courtney Pine and George Melly) can with our constant prattling on about blacks and whites sound just as racist as the racists. How can we help it? It's in the language; it's even in the thought-processes. You, my readers, and I, your author, are (naturally!) as sane as anyone can be; we have our feet firmly on the ground; and this is a very serious discussion, as serious as I can make it. But isn't it just a fraction deranged to divide people up according to their *skin colour*? Think about it. Because that's exactly what anti-racists have to do if they are to take a stand against racism. Consider such things as positive discrimination policies and black collectives; consider, even, the formulation I've used myself above – that racism is a white problem and not a black one.

Chronology

1934 Born 26 September, 6.30p.m. I'm told. Same birthday as George Gershwin, T.S. Eliot, Barnes Wallis, Olivia Newton-John, Bryan Ferry.

1939 Parents moved to Hengwm Hill Farm, Whitton, Knighton, Radnorshire. Went to village school in Whitton.

1946 Went for one term to Bootham School, York. Put foot down, refused to go back.

1947 Parents moved to Jasmine Cottage, Duffus, near Elgin, Morayshire. Went to school at nearby Gordonstoun for five years. Clarinet lessons with Frau Suzanne Lachmann; Mozart's 39th (Trio of Minuet and Trio) first music I played. Seized with passionate illicit interest in (a) Pee Wee Hunt's '12th Street Rag' and (b) Benny Goodman's 'Bach Goes to Town'.

1949 Father quarrelled with Gordonstoun headmaster Kurt Hahn about Hahn's espousal of Plato's recommendation that leaders of society should lie. Moved to caravans on Dartington Estate near Totnes, Devon. Went to Foxhole School, Dartington, September '49. Clarinet lessons with William Wraighty; persuaded father to buy Boosey & Hawkes alto saxophone, £25. Fellow pupil was Black American Kaye Dunham (nephew of Katherine Dunham, dancer); he understood jazz and thought I had a feel for it, persuaded me to play at informal school get-togethers. Discovered Sidney Bechet; persuaded father to buy Maltese soprano saxophone, £10. Became leader of school jazz band, upholding Bechet against Bunk Johnson and George Lewis, Johnny Dodds against Jimmie Noone, etc. Left Christmas 1952.

1953   January–August: tractor driver for John McElderry, Merrifield Farm, South Brent, Devon. September: went to Sidney Sussex College, Cambridge, as agricultural student. Did minimum of academic work, maximum of jazz.

1954   Became co-leader of University Jazz Band.

1955   Won silver cup (!) for playing good solo in front of judge Sandy Brown at Inter-University Jazz Contest; performance later issued on LP.

1956   Left Cambridge with degree. Led University Jazz Band on tour of Swiss jazz venues. Moved to London to do National Service, portering in hospital.

1957   Back injury ended National Service. Became professional jazz musician. Went from thirteen stone to ten and a half in five months. December: joined Sandy Brown's Jazz Band.

1958   Joined Ronnie Smith Quintet to do eighteen-week season at Butlin's, Filey.

1959   Freelanced. All sorts, including touring Europe in the pit with Jerome Robbins's Ballets USA; nightclub work; jazz one-nighters; jazz-club residencies; Bert Courtley Sextet; Flamingo All-Niters; New Departures Jazz'n'Poetry gigs.

1962   June–July: joined Alexis Korner's Blues Incorporated.

1963   August: joined Graham Bond, Ginger Baker and Jack Bruce to form Graham Bond Organization.

1967   July: joined John Mayall's Bluesbreakers.

1968   August: founder member of Jon Hiseman's Colosseum.

1971   November: Colosseum folded.

1972   March–April: made solo album *A Story Ended*. July–August: formed Manchild. October: toured UK with Manchild. November–December: toured USA with Manchild.

1973   March–April: recording of Manchild's first album inter-
        rupted by severe back injury. May–September: con-
        valescence. October: went to Polytechnic of the South
        Bank to study for BSc in Social Sciences.
1976   June: obtained BSc. Applied to London School of
        Economics to do postgraduate research. October: began
        M.Phil. at LSE. Began to gig with Big Chief.
1977   M.Phil converted to PhD. Continued to gig; Big Chief;
        Tough Tenors, etc.
1979   Social Science Research Council discontinue grant.
        Research not completed. Gigs continue: Big Chief,
        occasional jazz clubs, occasional appearances with
        semi-pro blues band the Famous Blues Blasters.
1980   Gigs as 1979.
1981   Famous Blues Blasters turn pro, become Mainsqueeze.
        Tours of UK, Scandinavia, Germany, France (even).
1982   Mainsqueeze continues.
1983   Mainsqueeze links up with Bo Diddley for European
        and UK tours.
1984   Mainsqueeze quietly ceases to work in September.
        Discussions with guitarist John James result in forma-
        tion of 3-Space, guitar–sax–keyboards trio.
1985   3-Space tours part-time.
1986   3-Space breaks up. I form new group, Matt Black; join
        African group, Julian Bahula's Electric Dream and work
        with many groups, including Electric Dream (1987),
        Matt Black, Mike Reinhardt Sextet (BRD).

Discography

The following discography is meant to be a general guide to the recordings of Dick Heckstall-Smith, not a detailed discography of each group with which he has worked. I have therefore not attempted to list every known issue worldwide and in some cases have noted only a collective personnel. There may also be recordings where Dick worked as a session musician which he has forgotten and I have not been able to trace. I would like to acknowledge the help given to me in compiling this discography by Alan Newby, Dick Heckstall-Smith, the Decca Record Company and the National Sound Archive. Except where noted all venues/locations are London, England and all records are issued in the UK.

Abbreviations: a = arranger; as = alto sax; bg = bass guitar; bjo = banjo; bs = baritone sax; cl = clarinet; g = guitar; hm = harmonica; key = keyboards; org = organ; p = piano; ss = soprano sax; tb = trombone; tp = trumpet; ts = tenor sax; vcl = vocal; vln = violin.

Tony Middleton

1956:
Saturday,
21 June

SANDY BROWN'S JAZZ BAND
Al Fairweather (tp); John R.T. Davies (tb); Sandy Brown (cl); Dick Heckstall-Smith (ss); Alan Thomas (p); Moe Umansky (bjo); Brian Parker (b); Graham Burbidge (d).

V0G878   **My Neck of the Woods**   Tempo TAP 3
Note: other titles do not feature Dick Heckstall-Smith.

Monday, *20 August*	DICK HECKSTALL-SMITH QUINTET Dick Heckstall-Smith (ss); Sandy Brown (cl); Dill Jones (p); Major Holley (b); Don Lawson (d). **Fish Man** Nixa NJE 1037 **Monochrome** — Note: other titles do not feature Dick Heckstall-Smith. NJE 1037 title 'Very Special Old Jazz'.

1957:

Thursday, *19 September*	DICK HECKSTALL-SMITH QUARTET Dick Heckstall-Smith (ss); Dave Stevens (p); Tim Mahn (b); Maurice Price (d). **Out of Nowhere** 77 EP13 **Aunt Hager's Blues** — **Pennies from Heaven** — **Four or Five Times** —
Wednesday, *25 September*	BOB WALLIS AND THE STORYVILLE JAZZMEN Bob Wallis (tp, vcl); Mac Duncan (tb); Acker Bilk (cl); Dick Heckstall-Smith (ss); Hugh Rainey (bjo); Bill Reid (b); Ginger Baker (d). **High Society** 77 LEU12/1 **Tartan Socks** — Note: Dick Heckstall-Smith may be on other titles from the above session which took place at Ken Coyler's Club. 77 LEU12/1 title 'Acker's Early Days'.
Wednesday, *30 October*	DICK HECKSTALL-SMITH QUINTET Dick Heckstall-Smith (ss); Bruce Turner (as); Harry Smith (p); Brian Brocklehurst (b); Eddie Taylor (d). **Lover Man** Nixa NJL 20 **Russian Lullaby** Nixa NJT 510
Thursday, *5 November*	as previous except Sandy Brown (cl) replaces Bruce Turner. **Sputnik** Nixa NJT 510 **There'll Never be** **Another You** — Note: other titles do not feature Dick Heckstall-Smith. NJL 20 title 'Blackstick'. NJT 510 title 'Jazz Gumbo Vol.2'.

1962:

Friday, *8 June*		ALEXIS KORNER'S BLUES INCORPORATED Dick Heckstall-Smith (ts); Keith Scott (p); Alexis Korner (g); Spike Heatley (b); Graham Burbidge (d); Cyril Davies (hm, vcl); Long John Baldry (vcl).
	DR29315	**I Wanna Put a Tiger in** **Your Tank vCD** Ace of Clubs ACL 1130
	DR29316	**Trouble No More** unissued
	DR29317	**Down Home** Ace of Clubs ACL 1130
	DR29318	**I Thought I Heard that** **Train Whistle Blow** **vLJB** —

DR29319	**Rain is Such a Lonesome Sound vLJB**	—
DR29320	**Keep Your Hands Off vCD**	—
DR29321	**Times are Getting Tough**	unissued
DR29322	**I'm Built for Comfort**	unissued
DR29323	**How Long, How Long Blues vLJB**	Ace of Clubs ACL 1130
DR29324	**Hoochie Coochie Man vCD**	—
DR29325	**Gotta Move**	—
DR29326	**I Got My Brand on You vCD**	—
DR29327	**I Got My Mojo Working**	—
DR29328	**Finkel's Cafe**	—
DR29329	**I Feel So Good**	unissued
DR29330	**Spooky But Nice**	Ace of Clubs ACL 1130

Note: ACL 1130 title 'Rhythm and Blues from the Marquee'.

1963:
Summer

ALEXIS KORNER'S BLUES INCORPORATED
Dick Heckstall-Smith (ts); Art Themen (as, ts); Johnny Parker (p); Alexis Korner (g, bouzouki); Mike Scott (b); Phil Seamen (d).

XDR34568	**Blue Mink**	Ace of Clubs ACL 1187
XDR34569	**Rainy Tuesday**	—
XDR34570	**Yogi**	—
XDR34571	**Sappho**	—
XDR34572	**Navy Blue**	—
XDR34573	**Royal Dooji**	—
XDR34574	**Preachin' the Blues**	—
XDR34575	**The Captain's Tiger**	—
XDR34576	**A Little Bit Groovy**	—
XDR34577	**Anything for Now**	—
XDR34578	**Chris Trundle's Habit**	—
XDR34579	**Trundlin'**	—

Note: master numbers probably assigned in December 1964.

1964:
Monday,
16 March

ALEXIS KORNER'S BLUES INCORPORATED
Dave Castle (as); Dick Heckstall-Smith, Art Themen (ts); Ron Edgeworth (org); Alexis Korner (g); Danny Thompson (b); Barry Howton (d).

Skippin'	Transatlantic TRA 117
Herbie's Tune	—
Chicken Shack	—

Note: other titles do not feature Dick Heckstall-Smith. TRA 117 title 'Red Hot from Alex'.

	THE GRAHAM BOND ORGANIZATION	
Tuesday, *5 May*	Dick Heckstall-Smith (ts); Graham Bond (org, vcl); Jack Bruce (b); Ginger Baker (d).	
DR33258	**Long Legged Baby**	Decca F11909, LK 4616, TAB 54
DR33259	**Hoochie Coochie Man**	Decca Roots 6, LK 4616, TAB 54
DR33260	**Long Tall Shorty**	Decca F11909, DPA 3009, TAB 54

Note: other tracks do not feature Graham Bond. DPA 3009 is part of a double LP DPA 3009/10 title 'Hard Up Heroes'.

	THE GRAHAM BOND ORGANIZATION	
May	Dick Heckstall-Smith (ts); Graham Bond (org, vcl); Jack Bruce (b); Ginger Baker (d).	
DR33290	**Strut Around**	Decca LK 4616
DR33291	**Hi Heel Sneakers**	— , Roots 6, Tab 88
DR33292	**Little Girl**	—

Note: other tracks do not feature Graham Bond. LK 4616 title 'Rhythm and Blues'.

	THE GRAHAM BOND ORGANIZATION	
Thursday, *6 August*	as previous.	
DR33793	**Wade in the Water**	Decca LK 4681
DR33794	**I Want You**	unissued

Note: other tracks do not feature Graham Bond. LK 4681 title 'Blues Now'.

GONKS GO BEAT
A 'Titan' feature film in which the Graham Bond Organization (personnel as previous) play one number HARMONICA, probably recorded for the soundtrack in August 1964, issued by Decca, with master number assigned in September 1964.

	THE GRAHAM BOND ORGANIZATION	
August/ *September*	as previous.	
DR34583	**Harmonica**	Decca LK 4673

Note: other tracks do not feature Graham Bond. LK 4673 title 'Gonks Go Beat'.

	THE GRAHAM BOND ORGANIZATION	
October	Dick Heckstall-Smith (ts); Graham Bond (org, as, vcl); Jack Bruce (bg); Ginger Baker (d).	
	Wade in the Water	Charly CR30198
	Big Boss Man	—
	Early in the Morning	—
	Person to Person Blues	—
	Spanish Blues	—
	introduction by Dick Jordan	

	The First Time I Met the Blues	—		
	Stormy Monday	—		
	Train Time	—		
	What'd I Say	—		

Note: recorded live at Klook's Kleek Club. CR 30198 title 'The Beginning of Jazz-Rock'. All titles issued in France on BYG 52903, 52904.

late 1964		THE GRAHAM BOND ORGANIZATION		
		as previous.		
7XCA28100	Tammy	Columbia DB 7471, 33SX1711		
7XCA28101	Wade in the Water	—	—	
	Hoochie Coochie	—		
	Baby Make Love to Me	—		
	Neighbour Neighbour	—		
	Early in the Morning	—		
	Spanish Blues	—		
	Oh Baby	—		
	Little Girl	—		
	I Want You	—		
	Got My Mojo Working	—		
	Train Time	—		
	Baby be Good to Me	—		
	Half a Man	—		

Note: title 'The Sound of '65'.

1965:

early 1965

as previous.

Tell Me	Columbia DB 7528
Love Come Shining Through	—

middle 1965

as previous.

Lease on Love	Columbia DB 7647
My Heart's in Little Pieces	—

late 1965

THE GRAHAM BOND ORGANIZATION
Dick Heckstall-Smith (ts, bs); Graham Bond (org, as, vcl, mellotron); Jack Bruce (bg, hm, vcl); Ginger Baker (d).

Who's Afraid of Virginia Woolf?	Columbia 33SX1750
Hear Me Calling Your Name	—
The Night Time is the Right Time	—
Walkin' in the Park	—
Last Night	—
Baby Can It Be True?	—
What'd I Say	—
Dick's Instrumental	—

Don't Let Me Go	—
Keep A'Drivin'	—
Have You Ever Loved a	
Woman?	—
Camels and Elephants	—

Note: title 'There's a Bond Between Us'.

1966:
early 1966

THE GRAHAM BOND ORGANIZATION
as previous.

St. James Infirmary	Columbia DB 7838
Soul Tango	—

middle 1966

THE GRAHAM BOND ORGANIZATION
Dick Heckstall-Smith (ts, ss); Graham Bond (org, as, vcl, p); Jon Hiseman (d).

Green Onions	Warner Brothers WS3001, K66004
Springtime in the City	—
Can't Stand It	—
Sweet Sixteen	—
Last Night	—
Long Legged Baby	—
Walkin' in the Park	—
It's Not Goodbye	—
Neighbour Neighbour	—

Note: other titles, recorded in June 1963, do not feature Dick Heckstall-Smith. Title 'Solid Bond'.

late 1966

THE GRAHAM BOND ORGANIZATION
Dick Heckstall-Smith (ts, ss); Graham Bond (key, vcl); Jon Hiseman (d).

You Gotta Have Love Baby	Page One POF 014
I Love You	—

1967:
Thursday, 14 September

JOHN MAYALL'S BLUESBREAKERS
Brass; reeds including Dick Heckstall-Smith (ts, ss, as); Chris Mercer (ts, bs); John Mayall (g); Mick Taylor (g); Paul Williams (b); Keef Hartley (d).

DR41355	Suspicions (part one) aDHS	Decca F 12684, SKL 5086
DR41356	Suspicions (part two) aDHS	Decca F 12684, SKL 5010

Note: SKL 5010 title 'Looking Back'. SKL 5086 title 'Thru the Years'.

Thursday, 19 October Newcastle

JOHN MAYALL'S BLUESBREAKERS
Dick Heckstall-Smith (ts, ss); Chris Mercer (ts, bs); John Mayall (g, hm, p, vcl); Mick Taylor (g); Paul Williams (b); Keef Hartley (d).

DR41922	Blood on the Night	Decca LK 4918, SKL 4918

Thursday,	as previous except Keith Tillman (b) replaces Paul	
2 November	Williams.	
DR41926	**My Own Fault**	Decca LK 4918, SKL 4918
DR41932	**Blues in Bb**	Decca LK 4919, SKL 4919
Sunday,		
5 November		
Schiedam Holland		
DR41924	**I Can't Quit You Baby**	Decca LK 4918, SKL 4918
DR41925	**Anzio Annie (excerpt)**	— —
Monday,		
13 November		
Belfast		
DR41925	**Snowy Wood (excerpt)**	Decca LK 4918, SKL 4918
Tuesday,		
14 November		
Port Stewart		
DR41927	**God Save the Queen**	Decca LK 4918, SKL 4918
Sunday,		
26 November		
Nottingham		
DR41931	**Help Me**	Decca LK 4919, SKL 4919
Tuesday,		
28 November		
Southampton		
DR41928	**Gimme Some Lovin/**	Decca LK 4919, SKL 4919
	The Train	
Thursday,		
7 December		
Colchester		
DR41933	**Soul of a Short Fat Man**	Decca LK 4919, SKL 4919
Tuesday,		
12 December		
DR41925	**The Lesson (excerpt)**	Decca LK 4918, SKL 4918
Tuesday,		
19 December		
DR41929	**Crying Shame**	Decca LK 4919, SKL 4919

Note: 4918 title 'The Diary of a Band' Vol 1. 4919 title 'The Diary of a Band' Vol 2. LPs also include speech tracks.

December	JOHN MAYALL'S BLUESBREAKERS	
	as previous.	
DR41934	**Jenny**	Decca F 12732, SKL 5010
DR41935	**Picture on the Wall**	— —

Note: SKL 5010 title 'Looking Back'.

1968:

3, 9, 24 & 30 April   JOHN MAYALL'S BLUESBREAKERS
Henry Lowther (tp, vln); Dick Heckstall-Smith (ts, ss); Chris Mercer (ts, bs); John Mayall (g, hm, vcl, org, harpsichord); Mick Taylor (g, hawaiian g); Tony Reeves (b, bg); Jon Hiseman (d, percussion).

DR42656	I'm a Stranger	Decca LK 4965, SKL 4965
DR42657	No Reply	— — , F12792
DR42658	Hartley Quits	— —
DR42659	Killing Time	— —
DR42660	She's Too Young	— — —
DR42661	Sandy	— —
DR42662	Bare Wires	— —
	Where Did I Belong	— —
	Start Walking	— —
	Fire	— —
	I Know How	— —
	Look in the Mirror	— —
DR48830	Knockers Step Forward (April 24)	Decca SKL 5086
DR48831	Hide and Seek (April 30)	—

Note: 4965 title 'Bare Wires'. 5086 title 'Thru the Years'.

Saturday, 25 May Brighton   JOHN MAYALL'S BLUESBREAKERS
Henry Lowther (tp); Dick Heckstall-Smith (ss); Chris Mercer (ts); John Mayall (g, hm, vcl, org); Mick Taylor (g); Tony Reeves (bg); Jon Hiseman (d).
(Intro) **Look at the Girl**   Decca TAB 66
Start Walkin'   —
Note: other titles on TAB 66 title 'Primal Scream', do not feature Dick Heckstall-Smith.

August   JACK BRUCE
Dick Heckstall-Smith (ts, ss); Jack Bruce (b); Jon Hiseman (d).
Over the Cliff   Polydor 234033
Statues   —

add John McLaughlin (g).
Sam Enchanted Dick
  (Medley)
  a. **Sam's Sack;**
  b. **Rill's Thrills**   —
Hckhh Blues   —
Ballad for Arthur   —
Things We Like   —
Note: title 'Things We Like'.

17 & 18 September   THE NEW JAZZ ORCHESTRA
Derek Watkins, Henry Lowther, Harold Beckett (tp); Ian Carr (tp, flugelhorn); John Mumford, Michael Gibbs, Derek Wadsworth or Tony Russell (tb); George

Smith (tuba); Barbara Thompson (as, ss, flute); Dave Gelly (ts, cl, bass cl); Jim Philip (ts, cl, flute); Dick Heckstall-Smith (ts, ss); Frank Ricotti (vibes, marimba); Jack Bruce (b); Jon Hiseman (d); Neil Ardley (director).

Le Dejeuner sur l'herbe	Verve VLP 9236, SVLP 9236	
Naima	—	—
Angle	—	—
Ballad	—	—
Dusk Fire	—	—
Nardis	—	—
Study	—	—
Rebirth	—	—

Note: title 'Le Dejeuner sur l'herbe'.

1969:

Late 1968/
early 1969

COLOSSEUM
Henry Lowther (tp)-1; Dick Heckstall-Smith (ts, ss); Dave Greenslade (org, vcl); James Litherland (g, vcl); Tony Reeves (bg); Jon Hiseman (d).

Walking in the Park-1	Fontana STL 5510
Plenty Hard Luck	—
Mandarin	—
Debut	—
Beware the Ides of March	—
The Road She Walked Before	—
Those About to Die	—

(1st session, **Backwater Blues**)
Note: Jim Roche (g) replaces James Litherland on 'Backwater Blues'. STL 5510 title 'Those Who are About to Die Salute You'.

Early 1969

PETE BROWN AND HIS BATTERED ORNAMENTS
including Dick Heckstall-Smith (saxes); Chris Spedding (g).

7XCE21278	**The Week Looked Good on Paper**	Parlophone R 5767
7XCE21279	**Morning Call**	—

Spring/
summer 1969

COLOSSEUM
Dick Heckstall-Smith (ts, ss); Dave Greenslade (org, vcl, p, vibes); James Litherland (g, vcl); Tony Reeves (bg); Jon Hiseman (d); string quartet-1; brass section-2; Neil Ardley (a, director).

The Kettle	Vertigo VO 1, Bronze Help 4	
Elegy-1	—	—
Butt's Blues-2	—	—
The Machine Demands a Sacrifice	—	—

The Valentyne Suite
(Theme One –
January's Search;
Theme Two –
February's Valentyne;
Theme Three – The
Grass is Always
Greener . . .)   —   —
Note: 'The Kettle' features only a trio (Litherland, Reeves and Hiseman). VO 1 title 'The Valentyne Suite'.

Late 1969

COLOSSEUM
as previous except omit brass and strings, Dave Clempson (g, vcl) replaces James Litherland.
Bolero   Bronze/Island
                             ILPS 9173

The Grass is Greener   —

1970:
Early 1970

COLOSSEUM
as previous plus Chris Farlowe (vcl) – overdubbed July 1971.
Jumpin' off the Sun   Bronze/Island
  vCF   ILPS 9173
**Rope Ladder to the
  Moon**   —
Note: ILPS 9173, title 'The Collector's Colosseum', also contains tracks from STL 5510.

Summer 1970

COLOSSEUM
Dick Heckstall-Smith (ts, ss, spoken word-1); Dave Greenslade (org, vcl, p, vibes); Dave Clempson (g, vcl); Mark Clarke (bg); Jon Hiseman (d, percussion); Chris Farlowe (vcl).
**Theme for an
  Imaginary Western**   Vertigo 6360017
Down Hill & Shadows   —

add Barbara Thompson (saxes).
**Three Score and Ten,
  Amen-1**   —

add Harold Beckett (tp, flugelhorn); Derek Wadsworth (tb); two violins, two celli, one viola; Neil Ardley (a, director). Louis Cennamo (bg) replaces Mark Clarke.
Time Lament   Vertigo 6360017
The Daughter of Time   —

omit brass, strings, Chris Farlowe.
**Take Me Back to
  Doomsday**   —

omit Barbara Thompson.
Bring Out Your Dead   —

July *Royal Albert Hall*	as previous.

The Time Machine Vertigo 6360017
Note: title 'The Daughter of Time is Truth'.

1971:
March
Manchester/
Brighton

COLOSSEUM
Dick Heckstall-Smith (ts, ss); Dave Greenslade (org, vibes); Dave Clempson (g, vcl); Mark Clarke (bg, vcl); Jon Hiseman (d); Chris Farlowe (vcl).

Rope Ladder to the Moon	Bronze/Island ICD 1
Walking in the Park	—
Skelington	—
Tanglewood '63'	Bronze/Island ICD 2
Encore . . . **Stormy Monday Blues**	—
Los Angeles	—

1972:
March/April
Oxfordshire

DICK HECKSTALL-SMITH
Dick Heckstall-Smith (ts, ss, electronic soprano); Dave Greenslade, Gordon Beck (p); Graham Bond (p, org, vcl, moog synthesizer); Chris Spedding, Caleb Quaye (g); Mark Clarke (bg, vcl); Rob Tait (d); Jon Hiseman (d, congas, bongos, maraccas); Paul Williams, Chris Farlowe (vcl).

Future Song	Bronze/Island ILPS 9196
Crabs	—
Moses in the Bullrushourses	—
What the Morning was After	—
The Pirate's Dream	—
Same Old Thing	—

Note: the above is a collective personnel, the band differs on each title. ILPS 9196 title 'A Story Ended'.

1978:
April
Pinewood

ALEXIS KORNER AND FRIENDS
Mike Zwerin (tb, bass tpt); Dick Heckstall-Smith (as, ts, ss); Art Themen (ts, ss); Dick Morrissey (ts); Mel Collins (ts, ss, bs); John Surman (ss, bs, a); Zoot Money (electric p, vcl); Alexis Korner (g, vcl, a); Colin Hodgkinson (bg); Stu Speer (d).

Things ain't what They Used to Be	Intercord INT 170.000
Captain's Tiger	—
Skipping	—
Spoonful	—
Medley: **Finkle's Cafe**	—
Dooji Hooji	—

add Eric Clapton, Neil Ford (g); Paul Jones, Duffy
Power (hm); Chris Farlowe (vcl).

Hey Pretty Mamma	—
Hi-Heel Sneakers	—
Stormy Monday Blues	—

Note: Dick Heckstall-Smith is not on other titles from
this session. Title 'The Party Album'.

1980:
1980

BRIAN KNIGHT
including Dick Heckstall-Smith, Art Themen (saxes);
Ian Stewart (p); Peter Green (g); Charlie Watts, Micky
Waller (d); Brian Knight (vcl, hm, slide g).

Boogie Beat	PVK BRY 1
Goin' Down Slow	—
Bring Your Corn to Me	—
Trouble in Mind	—
Honey Bee	—
Blues is Rock 'n' Roll	—
Manish Boy	—
Got the Blues 4U	—
Good Morning Blues	—
Cabin in the Sky	—
Bright Lights Big City	—

Note: title 'A Dark Horse'.

1983:
Saturday,
15 January

MAINSQUEEZE
Dick Heckstall-Smith (as, ts, ss); Diana Wood (as, vcl);
Victor Brox (tp, vcl); Dave Moore (rhodes p, clavinet,
moog, roland org); Eric Bell (g, vcl); John O'Leary (hm,
congas); Keith Tillman (fender b); Stretch (d, percussion);
Rod Coombes (percussion).

Voodoo Man	Expulsion Exit 1
Frosty	—
You Can Have My Husband	—
Born in Chicago	—
Itch	—
Casting My Spell	—
Framed	—
Sweet Sixteen	—
The Creeper	—
Rock Me Baby	—
Hipshake	—

BO DIDDLEY with MAINSQUEEZE
Bo Diddley (g, vcl); Dick Heckstall-Smith (saxes); Dave
Moore (key); Eric Bell (g); Keith Tillman (bg); Stretch
(d).

Intro/Bo Diddley Vamp	Conifer CFRC 507
Doctor Jeckyll	—

Everleen —
I Don't Know Where
I've been —
You Can't Judge
a Book —
Roadrunner —
I'm a Man —
Mona —
Note: Title 'Hey . . . Bo Diddley in Concert'.

Dick Heckstall-Smith is on the following John James LP made in 1984: 'Acoustica Eclectica', Stoptime Records STOP 101.

1985:
Vicenza Italy

GUIDO TOFFOLETTI'S BLUES SOCIETY
Dick Heckstall-Smith (as, ts, ss); Zoot Money (org); Ian Stewart (p); Mick Taylor (g, slide g); Guido Toffoletti (vcl, g, slide g, hm, dobro); Massimo Fantinelli (bg); Massimo Iannantuono (d); Sappho Korner (vcl).
Forget that Girl   Appaloosa AP 048
Still the Same —
You Know the Reason
Why —
Try Just One More Time —
Woke Up this Mornin' —
I'm Walkin' Out the
Door —
Let Me Hold You Tight —
In and Out —
Let's Have Some Fun —
The Same Old Story —
Note: title 'No Compromise', LP issued in Italy.

DE LUXE BLUES BAND
Dick Heckstall-Smith (ts, ss); Danny Adler (g, v); Bob Hall (p); Bob Brunning (bg); Mickey Waller (d).
I Got the Blues   Appaloosa 122 060–1
Danny Jumps One —
I Get So Weary —
Alimony Blues —
Shake Your
Moneymaker —
Sunnyland —
I'll Change My Style —
The Sky is Crying —
Southern Country Boy —
Bleeding Heart —
Note: title 'Motorvating'.

Index

Adderley, Cannonball, 43
Advision Studios, 125
Africa, 150–1, 153
Airforce, 116
alcohol, 18–20, 24
'All Right Now', 122
amphetamines, 16–17, 19
Anderson, Ian, 114
Apple, 138
Ardley, Neil, 122
Armstrong, Louis, 149

Bach, J.S., 24, 135–6
'Bach Goes to Town', 145–6, 155
Bahula, Julian, 157
Bailey, Pete Junior, 50, 68, 70–1
Bailey, Pete Senior, 50, 68, 69, 82
Baker, Ginger, 29–30, 36; DH-S first meets, 13–15; drugs, 15, 24, 26; drums fall off bus, 30; and Blues Incorporated, 39–44;

Graham Bond Organization, 45, 49–55, 57, 156; Cream, 57; journey from Carlisle to Southampton, 58–64; leaves Graham Bond Organization, 65; Airforce, 116
Baker, Liz, 54
Bakerloo, 107
barbiturates, 17, 19
Barcelona, 49
Bare Wires, 96–7
Barefield, Eddie, 149
Basil Kirchin Small Band, 28
Bates, Colin, 4,5
Bath Festival, 106, 115
BBC, 137, 147
'Beale Street Blues', 147
Beard, Johnny, 28
Beatles, 114
bebop, 1–2
Bechet, Sidney, 1, 13, 147, 149, 150, 156
'Bechet's Creole Blues', 147

Beck, Gordon, 137
Bee Gees, 114
Beiderbecke, Bix, 150
Bernstein, Leonard, 29
Bert Courtley Sextet, 36–7, 156
Big Chief, 155
Blue Flames, 45, 105
Blue Lagoon, 29
'Blue 'n' Boogie', 38
'blues', 17
Blues Incorporated, 33–44, 45–9, 156, 159–60
Blues Society, 170
Bluesbreakers, 87–99, 100–1, 106, 115, 116–117, 156, 163–5
Bond, Graham, 31, 43–4, 45–6, 49–57, 58–9, 65–6, 68–80, 81–5, 94, 114, 137, 156
Bonzo Dog Doo Dah Band, 120
Boosey & Hawkes, 146, 155
Bootham School, York, 155
Bosley, Ernest, 4
Boston, 106
Bown, Vernon, 10
Boxall, Mr, 3, 4
Branson, Richard, 137
Bromel Club, Bromley, 51
Bron, Gerry, 102, 129, 135, 136, 138, 140
Bronze Records, 138
Broughton, Edgar, 119
Brown, Pete, 104, 129, 136–7
Brown, Sandy, 2, 7–10, 156, 158
Bruce, Jack, 38–40, 41, 43–4, 45, 49–50, 57, 104, 105, 122, 129, 136, 156, 165
Burch, Johnny, 15, 39, 57

Butlin's Holiday Camp, Filey, 10, 156

Cafe au GoGo, New York, 89–91
Cafe des Artistes, Redcliffe Gardens, 13, 29, 30
Cambridge University, 36–8, 156
Cambridge University Jazz Band, 46, 156
Cambridge University Jazz Club, 2, 41
Carlisle, 58–9
Charles, Ray, 24–6
'Cherokee', 33
Chicago, 139
Churchill, Sir Winston, 113
Clarke, Mark, 137
Clempson, Dave ('Clem'), 107, 123, 124, 125–6, 133, 137
cocaine, 20–2, 24, 27
Coleridge, Samuel Taylor, 75–6, 78
Colosseum, 102–8, 113, 114–23, 124–34, 135–7, 141, 156, 166–8
Colosseum Live, 121, 122
Coltrane, John, 134, 149
Colyer, Ken, 2
Comecon, 110, 112
Cork, 120
Courtley, Bert, 29, 36–7, 156
Cream, 57, 65, 136
Cropper, Steve, 149
Crowley, Aleister, 79
Czech Communist Party, 112, 113
Czechoslovakia, 107–13

Czernik, 112

Daily Mirror, 77
Dakis, Tony, 28
Daughter of Time, 117
Davies, Cyril, 35–6, 39, 40, 41,
  42–3, 48
Dawbarn, Bob, 114–15
De Luxe Blues Band, 170
Decca, 40
Deep Purple, 115, 125, 138
Dentith, John, 138, 140
Detroit, 106
Diddley, Bo, 157, 169–70
Dobell, Doug, 16
Dodds, Johnny, 149, 156
Dohnanyi, Ernst von, 146
Donne, John, 76
'Dooji Wooji', 40
Doubtful Schoolmaster, 22–3
drugs, 16–27, 72–3
Dubcek, Alexander, 111–12,
  113
Dunham, Katherine, 145, 155
Dunham, Kaye, 145, 146–7,
  148, 155–6

Ealing Club, 39
Electric Circus, New York, 107
Electric Dream, 157
Eliot, T.S., 75–6, 78, 137, 148,
  155
Elkington, Kris, 30–1
Escape Studios, 140
Exeter, 106

Fairweather, Al, 8
Faithfull, Marianne, 143
Falana, Mike, 50, 57, 58, 60–4,

68
Fame, Georgie, 15, 24, 44, 45,
  105, 112, 114
Famous Blues Blasters, 157
Farlowe, Chris, 117, 119, 120–
  1, 125, 137
Fehmarn, 116
Ferry, Bryan, 155
Fillmore West, San Francisco,
  93, 95, 106
Finland, 115–116
'Fire', 97
First World War, 22–3
Fishmonger's Arms, Wood
  Green, 87
Flamingo, Wardour Street ,
  15, 29, 39, 41, 44, 45, 91, 105,
  156
Fleetwood Mac, 138
Flick, Pete, 17, 19
Fosh, Eddie, 10
Foxhole School, Dartington, 1,
  146–7, 155
Frame, Peter, 124
Fraser, Andy, 96
Free, 96, 119, 122–3

Germany , 29–30, 113, 116,
  117–20, 122, 138
Gershwin, George, 155
Gibbs, Mike, 129
Gonks Go Beat, 161
Goodman, Benny, 145–6, 155
Gordonstoun, 155
Graham, Bill, 93, 106
Graham Bond Organization
  (GBO), 50–7, 58–64, 65–72,
  81–3, 86, 88–9, 95, 100, 126,
  156, 161–3

Grand Ballroom, Detroit, 106
Grant, Keith, 71, 72
Gray, Wardell, 1, 149
Greek Civil War, 113
Greenslade, Dave, 102, 119, 125, 126, 128, 137
Gunnell, John, 24
Gunnell, Rik, 13–14
Gunnell Agency, 98

Hahn, Kurt, 155
Haight Ashbury, 93–5
Harlem, 91
Hartley, Keef, 87, 96
'Hary Janos' Suite, 146
Hebden, Paul, 142–3
Heckstall-Smith, Arthur, 95
Heckstall-Smith, Gary, 8, 10–12, 95–6, 101
Heckstall-Smith, Hugh (father), 22–3, 53, 146, 147, 155–6
Hell's Angels, 116
Hendrix, Jimi, 114, 116
Henley, Don, 77
heroin, 20–2, 26, 27, 72–3
Hines, Earl, 40
Hiseman, Jon, 112; Graham Bond Organization, 50, 65–72, 81–2; in Bluesbreakers, 96, 97–9; Colosseum, 100–4, 106, 113, 114–16, 119, 120, 156; Colosseum breaks up, 123, 124–34; and *A Story Ended*, 136–8
Hogg, Derek, 8
Hoogenboom, Andy, 35, 39
Howard, Charlie, 34
Huckridge, Johnny, 37

Hughes, Glen, 16–17
Hunt, John, 83
Hunt, Pee Wee, 146, 155
Husak, Gustav, 113
Hymns Ancient and Modern, 151

IBC studios, 104, 106
Inter-University Jazz Contest, 2, 156
Irish Jim, 50
Israel, 29
Italy, 122

Jack, John, 103–4
Jackson, Eddie, 29, 91, 139
James, John, 157
Jerome Robbins Ballet USA, 29, 107, 156
Jethro Tull, 114
John Coltrane Quartet, 134
Johnny Burch Octet, 57
Johnny Burch Quartet, 15, 24, 39
Johnson, Bunk, 156
Johnson, Lonnie, 34
Johnson, Robin, 146
Jones, Elvin, 134, 149
Jones, Ronnie, 46
Joplin, Janis, 116–17

Ken Colyer Club, 13
King, Albert, 95, 106, 149
Kirchin, Basil, 28
Knight, Brian, 169
Korner, Alexis, 34–5, 39–44, 45–6, 48, 49, 51, 86, 116, 156, 159–60, 168–9
Kozak, Ashley, 28

Lacan, Jacques, 1
Lachmann, Suzanne, 155
Lambert, Kit, 65
Lanchester Polytechnic,
   Coventry, 122
Lawford, Mick, 97
Leadbelly, 34
Led Zeppelin, 120
Lee, Alvin, 114
Lewis, George, 156
Lightfoot, Terry, 4
Litherland, James, 103, 105,
   107, 138, 140
Live at the Flamingo, 24
Live at the Marquee, 40
London School of Economics,
   155
Los Angeles, 91–3, 106
'Lover Man', 38
Lowther, Henry, 96, 100
Lunt, Dave, 13
Luter, Claude, 147
Lyceum, London, 123

McElderry, John, 156
McGhee, Brownie, 34
McLaughlin, John, 104–5
Mainsqueeze, 157, 169–70
Manchester University, 121
Manchild, 156–7
Manfred (road manager), 50,
   58–64
Manor Studios, 137
Marmalade, 120
Marquee Club, 40, 41
Marriott, Steve, 123, 125, 133
Massachusetts, 106
Matt Black, 157
Mayall, John, 87–99, 100–1,

106, 114, 115, 116–17, 156,
   163–5
Melly, George, 149–50, 153
Melody Maker, 102, 114–15,
   116, 117–19
Mercer, Chris, 87–8, 90
Middlesbrough, 81–2
Mike Reinhardt Sextet, 157
Mogul Thrash, 107
Montreux Festival, 106
Morgan, Lee, 149
Morganfield, McKinley, 50
Morituri Te Salutant, 105–6
morphia, 22–3, 26
Mothers of Invention, 91
Mozart, W.A., 155
Mumford, John, 4, 8
'Muskrat Ramble', 147
Mussorgsky, Modest, 146
'My Ship', 33

National Front (NF), 152
National Service, 2–4, 156
Netherlands, 122
New Departures, 156
New Jazz Orchestra, 122, 165–
   6
New York, 89–91, 106–7, 120
New York Times, 113
Newton-John, Olivia, 155
Noone, Jimmie, 156
Norman, Jessye, 149
Norwich, 69–70
Novotny, 111, 112
Nucleus, Monmouth Street,
   15, 16, 31
Nuremberg, 120

O'Casey, Niall, 34, 147

Occult Secrets, 73–4
Olympic Studios, Barnes, 71–2
100 Club, 8, 104
Ostende, 120

Paice, Ian, 125
Parker, Charlie, 149
Parker, Johnny, 40, 44
'Pictures at an Exhibition', 146
Pine, Courtney, 149, 153
'The Pirate's Dream', 130, 137
Plato, 155
Plumpton Festival, 115
Plymouth, 106, 147
Poland, 110
Polydor Records, 71–2
Polytechnic of the South Bank, 83, 143, 155
Potter, Brian, 50
Prague, 107–8, 112, 113
Preludin, 16
Purbrook, Colin, 4, 37
Purcell, Henry, 24

Quaye, Caleb, 137

racism, 144–5, 148–54
Ravel, Maurice, 146
Reagan, Ronald, 107
Reece, Red, 45
Reeves, Tony, 96, 102
Reinhardt, Mike, 157
Rendell, Don, 43
Richardson, Colin, 102, 113
Roaring Twenties, Carnaby Street, 44
Robbins, Jerome, 29, 107, 156

Roche, Jim, 103, 105
Rolling Stones, 40
Rollins, Sonny, 149
Romano's, Gerrard Street, 28
Ronnie Smith Quintet, 156
'Rope Ladder to the Moon', 129
Rose, Dave, 138, 140
Round House, Wardour Street, 35
Royal Albert Hall, London, 115, 123, 125, 135
'Royal Garden Blues', 147
Rumania, 110
Russell, Pee Wee, 149

St Bartholomew's Hospital, 3–4
St John's College, Cambridge, 36–7
Salvat, Maurice, 37, 38
San Francisco, 93–5
Sanborn, David, 149
Sandy Brown Jazzmen, 8–10
Scandinavia, 97, 122, 125
Scott, Keith, 35, 40
Scott, Ronnie, 27
Seamen, Phil, 27, 45, 46
Shannon, River, 68
Shorter, Wayne, 149
Sidney Sussex College, Cambridge, 156
Sims, Zoot, 41
slave trade, 153
Sly and the Family Stone, 116
Smith, Billy, 138, 140
Smith, Chuck, 10
Smith, Col, 97
Smith, Harry, 8

Smith, Ronnie, 10, 156
Social Science Research
    Council, 157
Solid Bond, 72
South Bank Poly, 83, 143, 155
Southampton, 58–9
Soviet Union, 110, 112–13
Spanish Civil War, 113
Spedding, Chris, 137
'speed', 19, 20, 24
Stalin, Joseph, 112–13
Steppenwolf, 115
Stevens, Dave, 40
Stigwood, 57, 65, 104
Sting, 103
Stobart, Kathy, 37
A Story Ended, 83, 137–8, 156
Storyville Jazzmen, 159
Student, 112
Studio 51, Great Newport
    Street, 13
Sweden, 120
Switzerland, 120

T-Bone, 149
Tait, Rob, 137
'Tanglewood '63', 129
Tauber, Richard, 4
Taylor, Mick, 87, 100
Taylor, Mike, 65
Tel Aviv, 29
Ten Years After, 114
Terry, Sonny, 34
Themen, Art, 46, 140
'There Will Never be Another
    You', 33
Things We Like, 105
Thompson, Chris, 45–6
'Those About to Die', 128

3-Space, 157
'Tiger Rag', 147
Toffoletti, Guido, 170
Torkanowsky, Werner, 29
Tough Tenors, 157
Troubadour, Old Brompton
    Road, 15, 33–4
Turku Festival, 115–16
'12th Street Rag', 146, 155

Ungano's, New York, 106
Unit Four Plus Two, 120
United States of America, 74,
    89–95, 106–7, 113, 125, 127,
    138, 139, 151
US State Department, 107

Van Dyck Club, Plymouth,
    106

Wallis, Barnes, 155
Wallis, Bob, 13, 159
Walsh, Joe, 77
Warner Brothers, 72
Warsaw, 107
Warsaw Pact, 112–13
Waters , Muddy, 34, 149
Watts, Charlie, 35, 40
Waverley Hotel, New York,
    89–90
Weimar Republic, 113
Welch, Chris, 117–19, 122, 125
Whelan, Nick, 8
Whisky a GoGo, Los Angeles,
    91–2, 106
White, Josh, 34
Who, 65
'Wild Man Blues', 147
Williams, Paul, 87, 96, 137

Williams, Richard, 30

Wiseman, Jeremy, 34

Wolf, 149

Wraighty, William, 155

Yes, 115, 120

Young, Lester, 1, 149

Zappa, Frank, 91